Twayne's United States Authors Series

EDITOR OF THIS VOLUME

Lewis Leary

University of North Carolina, Chapel Hill

John Reuben Thompson

TUSAS 346

John Reuben Thompson

JOHN REUBEN THOMPSON

By GERALD M. GARMON
West Georgia College

TWAYNE PUBLISHERS
A DIVISION OF G. K. HALL & CO., BOSTON

Published in 1979 by Twayne Publishers,
A Division of G. K. Hall & Co.
All Rights Reserved

Printed on permanent/durable acid-free paper and bound
in the United States of America

First Printing

Library of Congress Cataloging in Publication Data

Garmon, Gerald M
John Reuben Thompson.

(Twayne's United States authors series ; TUSAS 346)
Bibliography: p. 165-68
Includes index.
1. Thompson, John Reuben, 1823-1873.
2. Authors, American—19th century—Biography.
PS3033.T4Z67   811'.5'2   79-15602
ISBN 0-8057-7284-7

Contents

About the Author

Gerald M. Garmon is an associate professor of English at West Georgia College of the University System of Georgia. He received his B.A. and M.A. from the University of Richmond in Virginia and his Ph.D. from Auburn University. He formerly taught at Virginia Commonwealth University (then Richmond Professional Institute), the University of Virginia, and North Carolina Wesleyan College. He is a member of the Modern Language Association, the South Atlantic Modern Language Association, the College English Association, and has been twice president of the Georgia-South Carolina College English Association. He has also been president of the local chapter of the American Association of University Professors.

His writings include articles on Edgar Allan Poe, Joseph Conrad, D. H. Lawrence, J. R. R. Tolkien, and William Faulkner among others. He has been chairman of one seminar on bibliography and two seminars on Tolkien at meetings of the Modern Language Association. He has chaired the session on Science Fiction and Fantasy at the South Atlantic Modern Language Association.

Preface

John Reuben Thompson's work in shaping the culture of the United States in general and the South in particular is so important and so extensive that it justifies renewed consideration and appraisal. His name and reputation were well sustained for more than fifty years after his death. His poems appeared regularly in anthologies, and his influence as an editor reached into countless corners of American literary thought. The works of those he encouraged likewise continued to be popular — and some still do today. But Thompson's name, which reached a brief zenith in the 1920s — when his collected poems (1920), and his essay *The Genius and Character of Edgar Allan Poe* were published (1929), and Joseph R. Miller wrote his dissertation on Thompson's place in Southern literature (1930) — has almost disappeared from all but the more inclusive literary surveys.

It seems Thompson spoke of himself with prophetic accuracy when he wrote to Dr. George W. Bagby of their mutual friend John M. Daniel, "[He] is the dead representative of a buried principle, the dumb champion of a lost cause, the inefficient type of a race now extinct, and all interest in him, his writings and his country has quite faded out. . . . The world's now indifferent to us, its pulses are languid at the recital of our brave deeds, and it receives with apathy anything we may address to it." Since that time, just after the Civil War, interest has greatly revived in the time and its spirit; for this reason, if no other, Thompson's place in history should be reviewed. Some of his accomplishments have been kept before the public. His work as editor of the *Southern Literary Messenger* was noted in B. B. Minor's history of that journal, and his work as literary editor of the *New York Evening Post* has been examined in Henry Nevin's history of the newspaper. More recently, J. Cutler Andrews, in his compendious *The South Reports the Civil War,* has written about Thompson as a reporter and wartime editor. But no biography or other book-length study of Thompson has been published prior to the present one.

Part of Thompson's diminished recognition is due, doubtless, to the fact that he was generally thought to be a supporter of Rufus Griswold in the dispute that arose over the reputation of Edgar Allan Poe. His testimony on Poe was discredited early in the twentieth century by John H. Whitty, whose 1917 edition of Poe's poetry charged that Thompson did not know Poe well and that his testimony was thought to be exaggerated. From that time on, though Thompson's name is often mentioned in works on Poe, he is given little credit. To Poe scholars generally Thompson has proved an embarrassment, best ignored.

In presenting Thompson's life I have relied heavily on quotation, much more heavily than I would normally do. But Thompson's life is not elsewhere well documented and, when he chose, he wrote well of himself and of the events of which he was a part. It is best, then, within reason, to let the reader become acquainted with the writer through his own words. For the same reasons that I have quoted much from his letters and diaries, I have quoted his poetry. The one edition of his collected poems is out of print and difficult to find, so I have tried to supply the reader with examples. Much of the quotation from others is also introduced because it is not generally available nor familiar even to students of American literature, except the specialist. For example, the credo of the London *Index* is a rare and little known statement; I, therefore, quote it in full because it is important and unique as a part of our Civil War history.

My inclusive approach will, I hope, result in a renewed interest in Thompson's poetry, and his roles as editor, mentor to young writers, and conciliatory agent in the bitterness that followed the Civil War. Finally, I believe that Thompson's letters and essays on Poe are important tools in Poe studies; as the circumstances surrounding those statements concerning Poe are explained, one emerges with a greater respect for Thompson's words. One sees in Thompson a writer who deserves respect for his place in the American tradition in literature and for his work as a fastidious artist and a compassionate observer of the human race.

Acknowledgments

I am indebted to the West Georgia College Learning Resources Committee for a faculty grant to help me start work on this book. I am indebted to the college and the University System for providing me with a quarter off with partial pay while writing the first draft of this book.

To the librarians of West Georgia for finding numerous works, I am thankful, and I single out Mrs. Betty Jobson, Miss Kathleen Hunt, Mrs. Sarah Rigg, and Miss Jan Ruskell. To Mrs. Susan Smith for her work with inter-library loan I give special thanks. To Dr. James Mathews, chairman of my department, I am grateful for his reading of the earliest draft, and Mrs. Mary Anne DeVillier, who labored over the manuscript, is due more than I can repay.

I owe much to my friend, colleague and wife, Dr. Lucille Garmon of the Physics Department, for her encouragement, support and love, without which I would not have cared to do anything.

Acknowledgement is made to the Library of the University of Virginia for permission to quote from the letters in the John R. Thompson Collection, and from Joseph R. Miller's dissertation, and to the Peabody Institute Library, Baltimore, Maryland, for permission to quote from the letters in the John Pendleton Kennedy Collection. Acknowledgment is also made to the Tennyson Library Collection in Lincoln, England for permission to quote from the unpublished diary of Lady Emily Tennyson, and to the Library of Congress for permission to quote from the letters in the Barton Harrison Collection.

Chronology

1823   John Reuben Thompson born in Richmond, Va. on October 23.

1836   Attended school in East Haven, Conn.

1840   Entered the University of Virginia: B.A. in chemistry in 1842.

1843   Returned to University to study law: law degree in 1845.

1847   Purchased the *Southern Literary Messenger,* became editor.

1848   Met Edgar Allan Poe who was visiting Richmond.

1849   Met Rufus Griswold, whom he defended in journalistic battle over Poe's reputation.

1850   Printed in *Messenger* the controversial article on Poe written by John M. Daniel.

1852   Wrote review of Harriet Beecher Stowe's *Uncle Tom's Cabin,* prompting Mrs. Stowe to respond with *A Key to Uncle Tom's Cabin.*

1853   Met William Makepeace Thackeray, who visited Richmond at Thompson's request.

1854   First visit to Europe; met Anne Thackeray.

1856   *Across the Atlantic* published, but edition was burned.

1860   Left *Southern Literary Messenger* to become editor of *Southern Field and Fireside* in Augusta, Georgia.

1861   Resigned *Southern Field and Fireside* and returned to Richmond.

1861-   Wrote for *Memphis Daily Appeal* under pseudonym of
1864   "Dixie"; edited *Southern Illustrated News* and *Richmond Record;* served as assistant secretary of state for Virginia and assistant state librarian; wrote war poetry; wrote letters for London *Index.*

1864   Went to London, edited the *Index.*

1865   Wrote for Heros Van Borke *Memoirs of the Confederate War for Independence.*

1866   Stayed with Alfred Lord Tennyson at Farringford, his home; returned to Richmond.

1868 Became literary editor of William Cullen Bryant's New York *Evening Post*.

1873 Died in New York, April 30.

1920 *Poems* edited by John S. Patton.

1929 *The Character and Genius of Edgar Allan Poe* published privately in Richmond.

CHAPTER 1

John Reuben Thompson

W HAT in his own times distinguished John Reuben Thompson from his colleagues was his ability to converse. He was, without a doubt, a highly entertaining and witty conversationalist, but almost nothing of his repartee has been preserved. Certainly it would have lacked the polish and cynical irreverence of Oscar Wilde's or the vigor and iconoclasm of Samuel Johnson's best talk. Thompson was, in most ways, very much in tune with his times, and his speech was primarily courteous, social, and gentlemanly. Edmund Clarence Stedman, a friend of his later years and a Northerner, wrote of him:

He was to me the connecting link between Poe's generation and my own. He was a poet, scholar, wit, and a gentleman in the finest sense of that word; always a fascinating companion and a loveable, affectionate friend, ever devoted to the cause of the South, but in such wise that we loved him the better for it.[1]

Thompson seems, from almost all reports, to have been the very paragon of a nineteenth-century Southern gentleman. For this reason alone some sample of his powers as a conversationalist, if available, would be interesting and informative. Of course, Thompson was much more than a conversationalist. He was, perhaps foremost, an entrepreneur of Southern literature, a poet, editor, critic, diarist, journalist, and letter writer. Indeed, many of his friends thought letter-writing was what he did best. John Esten Cooke, for one, urged Thompson in 1860 to "sit down and write me your impressions of Augusta, Georgia. Letters are your forte."[2] Among those who have written on Thompson's literary reputation, however, it has been his poetry and editorial work which has been most stressed. Here, Thompson's journalism and letter-writing will be given equal recognition, for he was, among the men of his age in

America, preeminently a man of letters, in all the best connotations of that term.

John Thompson, the elder, John Reuben's father, was born in New Hampshire on January 5, 1790. At twenty-one he left his home state and traveled south. In New York he met and married Miss Sarah Dyckman, a descendant of Jan Dyckman, who had settled in the New Amsterdam colony as early as 1660. From New York, John Thompson and his bride moved to Richmond, Virginia, at that time (ca. 1818) a small city with a population of about twenty thousand, where he opened a hat, cap, and fur store on the corner of Fourteenth and Main streets. In their rooms above the store, Mrs. Thompson gave birth to four children, one of whom, Virginia, died in infancy just two months before her only son, John Reuben, was born on October 23, 1823. Three children grew up together in the Thompson home: Susan, the oldest child, Sarah (who married Mr. R. S. Massie) and John [Reuben], who never married.[3]

Little information about the early life of the children is available, but they seem to have been part of a very happy, close family. Mr. Thompson did well in his business, and Mrs. Thompson seems to have been a particularly affectionate and efficient mother who impressed on her children her own love and consideration for her fellow man. Years later, Susan was to remind her brother, then ill in London, of their mother's goodness:

My thoughts travel back to many a stranger's bed, whose loneliness Ma helped to cheer and whose friendless poverty she did all in her power to lighten, and remembering the promise "cast thy bread upon the waters and thou shalt find it after many days" my faith is strong that you, although by God's blessing, not needing pecuniary aid, will, while a stranger in a foreign land, receive every kindness that your enfeebled condition may require.[4]

What the nature of Mrs. Thompson's kindness and aid to the poor and friendless was is not recorded, but her compassion was evidently extended in even greater measure to her family.

The Thompsons lived first above the store. As business improved, they moved into a house on Franklin Street, between Fourteenth and Fifteenth streets, about a block from the store; this was probably about 1830. In 1838, the eldest daughter, Susan, married her father's shop assistant, Henry W. Quarles, and a year later Mr. Thompson built two houses on Mayo Street, numbers 106 and 108. Here the Thompsons and Quarleses lived, side by side, for almost twenty years. In 1858, the Thompsons moved back to Franklin Street, between Eighth and Nineth streets; two years later they moved to 802 Leigh Street. It was from the house at Fifteenth and Franklin streets that the three children began their schooling. Young John walked approximately seven blocks to Tenth and Broad streets to the school of which Hawesworth and Wright were masters. What little we know of him as a child suggests that he was bookish, though popular with his classmates. His lifelong friend B. Johnson Barber recalled in later years,

We also say without exaggeration that literature marked him for her own from birth. I have often heard from the lips of his honored parents an account of his insatiate appetite for books from youth upwards, frequently neglecting those sports so charming and seductive to his companions for some new volume which had fallen into his hands, and always exhibiting a wonderful retention of the salient points of everything he read.[5]

Of himself as a child Thompson wrote almost nothing, either in his published works or existing private letters. One rare and brief glimpse of his early life and influences is in an essay he wrote for the *Southern Literary Messenger* in 1848:

If there is one writer of modern times to whom we feel a deeper sense of personal obligation than another, it is Charles Lamb. His very name is suggestive of delightful companionship in years gone by, when, with Elia in hand, we lay beneath old trees and forgot all things else, in the dreamy enjoyment of his exquisite fancies. How many dreary days within doors has he not beguiled, when the rain-drops pattered incessantly against the panes, and ennui would have marked us for her own, but for the inimitable dolleries, the happy descriptions, the touching pathos of Elia.[6]

Thompson's essay style always remained much in debt to Lamb's.

Whether it was because John Reuben spent too much of his time reading Lamb and too little on his school work, or whether it was because his parents wanted to provide a companion for Sarah, who was ready for a finishing school, the young Thompson was sent off in 1836 to a preparatory school conducted by a Mr. Rogers in East Haven, Connecticut. Here, he and his sister, who was attending Mrs. MacKenzie's finishing school in the same town, remained for only eleven months. It was here that Thompson wrote his first known poem. A girl of his own age, Fanny Ball — later the wife of his friend William Munford — wrote him asking for some lines for her album. He responded with a dozen:

> Dear lady, O, the task is mine
> To write in your album a line
> Or two, if that would please you more
> And if I could I'd write a score.
>   Dear Fanny, such a heavy task
> Of you I'm sure I'd never ask,
> For I declare it's rather hard
> To wake my sleepy, slumbering bard.
>   But as I've written a line or two
> I think I'll try to make that do.
> Pray do not treat it with contempt
> Remember, 'tis my first attempt.[7]

Returning from East Haven, John entered the newly opened Richmond Academy sometime around 1837 and graduated in the spring of 1840. In March of that year the *Richmond Whig and Advertiser,* in a brief review of the school, noted a resolution passed by the students expressing their respects for a deceased classmate; John R. Thompson acted as secretary for the class.

In the fall of the same year he entered the University of Virginia, "at the beginning of his eighteenth year and the University's seventeenth session."[8] The University of Virginia in the mid-1800s was an exciting place to be. It had been designed, architecturally and academically by Thomas Jefferson as an academic village where students and tutors lived and worked side by side. When Thompson entered, it had just twelve professors and one hundred-seventy-nine students, but some of these professors were exceptionly fine scholars. He studied ancient languages under Gessner Harrison, famous in his time as one of America's outstanding linguists. He studied natural philosophy under William Rogers, among whose other accomplishments was founding the Massachusetts Institute of Technology. He studied mathematics under J. J. Sylvester, who later became the first incumbent of the chair of mathematics at Johns Hopkins University and then Savilean Professor of Geometry at Oxford.

The University was also a place of rebellion, riot, drinking, gaming, and insubordination. Its earliest days had been marred by student rebellion, followed by a period of calm during which the students were put on their honor as gentlemen to conduct themselves more mannerly. This proved none too successful, and the rules, which had to do with conduct, dress, debts, and class attendance proved to be more of a source of annoyance than an effective corrective, reappeared. Students became even more demonstrative. During the 1840-1841 school year, when Thompson entered, student resistance reached its height. Secret clubs, whose object it was to resist the new rules, had come into being, and the members nightly paraded on the grounds and disturbed the peace. Finally, a demonstration resulted in the death of a faculty member. The entire community was shocked and the clubs disappeared. The next year was comparatively quiet.[9]

Thompson is not known to have taken part in the student riots. He was, however, a rather indifferent student, reported by his professors at almost every faculty meeting as one of those who had "absented themselves too often from classes." He was also negligent about wearing the prescribed uniform on the grounds of the University, though he seems to have sported about in uniform gladly enough while on vacations. In April of 1841 Thompson was reported as "doing very little" in mathematics. In 1841, however, he made distinguished marks on the final examinations in natural philosophy and mathematics, graduating with a degree in chemistry and returning to Richmond in July, with a reputation as an accomplished linguist. Evidently, much of his time had been taken up with reading in German and French as well as in English.

Of ancient languages, however, he seems to have had little interest, if we may judge by his "Verses of a Collegiate Historian," written during his last days at the University.

> End at last! Gloria in Excelsis!!
> Eight minutes of eleven o'clock, Jan. 30th, 1841.
> Farewell! farewell to thee old Latin History!
> (Thus warbled a student, who once read it through.)
> Thou art so profoundly enveloped in mystery
>   That with feeling of pleasure I bid you adieu.
>
> Old Niebuhr no longer shall act as my teacher.
>   Researches like his are too boring for me.
> For though he has tales of "poetical nature,"
>   Yet poetry in them I never could see.
>
> "The Library for the diffusion of knowledge" —

> To give my opinion — a *humbug* I'll call.
> I hope that it soon will be kicked out of College
> "Etruscans," "Pelagi," "Venetians" and all.
>
> Old Rome's institutions, religious and civil,
> I leave with emotion unmixed with regret.
> And now Latin History may go to the d—l
> But the troubles it cost me I'll never forget.[10]

In addition to his conduct in classes, the records of the University reveal several miscellaneous bits of information about Thompson. He roomed, apparently by himself, in No. 49 West Lawn, and spent, for his room an average amount for a student at this time, thirty-one dollars a year. The five dollars a month his father sent as an allowance seems to have been enough, for he was charged with no delinquent bills. A member of the Jefferson Society, a literary club, he contributed seven poems to the college magazine in his two years as an undergraduate.

For some reason he had little to do with the magazine during his second year, when he had only two poems printed. In 1849, he wrote for the *Southern Literary Messenger* a brief history of the magazine which offers further evidence that he was not connected with it in his second year:

Eleven years ago, the students of our State University put forth a modest little *brochure* under the title of "The Collegian." The design of it was similar to that of the Eton boys in Mr. Canning's time as exhibited in the Etonian, — to furnish the undergraduates with an opportunity for practice in the art of English composition. *The Collegian* was born under the fairest auspices and continued for the space of four years to publish, every month during the term time, 32 pages of printed matter, wherein the young gentlemen of the institution were encouraged to write didactic essays, sentimental love-tales and verses such as Horace and the *Edinburgh Review* have united in condeming. At the end of the fourth year, however, without any premonition of approaching death and without one word by way of valedictory, *The Collegian* suddenly expired, regretted by a very small circle of friends.[11]

There is, however, one other little poem, written during this period which has not previously been published. It is addressed to Maria L. Dabney (later Mrs. William Cabell Carrington), and dated May 24, 1842, from No. 49 Western [*sic*] Lawn.

> You bid me wake my slumbering muse
> And soar for awhile on the pinions of song
> A lady's command I can never refuse,
> And so to Parnassus I hurry along.
>
> You have given me lady a fragrant bouquet,
> An offering meet for a worthier bard.
> Now if you will promise to smile on my lay
> I assure you 'twill be a sufficient reward.[12]

The only other matter of a literary nature with which Thompson's name was connected in his second year had to do with an invitation to Charles Dickens, who was to visit Richmond. Thompson received permission to invite Dickens to Charlottesville as well. Mr. Dickens declined the invitation.[13]

Thompson's surviving letters and essays reveal little further of his collegiate life. One interesting exception is his essay "The Theory of the Toilet," in which he wrote about the proprieties of dress and, in so doing, revealed something of his own life and influences. He saw, for example, the man who dresses well as a "true artiste":

> We mean not the man, who makes his wardrobe the serious business of his life, nor yet the recognized model of the fashionable world; he is but a pretender, and patent-leather can never raise him above his proper sphere. But there are some gifted individuals, who come into the world with a nice sense of the harmony of colors and the proprieties of the toilet who first evince a just perception of the true and becoming in dress by the jackets of their boyhood and who afterwards remain faultless in appearance. One such there was who cast a lustre on our college days. Very fair in the eye of memory, oh! Dr. —, is thy pleasant face, with its delicate fringe of whisker and its benignant smile! We well recollect the mingled feelings of envy and admiration with which we were wont to regard his exceeding propriety in every movement and under all circumstances, whether attired in white cravat and lemon-colored kids for an evening, or difused upon the grass, in gown and slippers, with a fragrant Havana, or preparing the first of the vernal juleps, or making the lawn vocal with his midnight guitar![13]

Thompson evidently thought of himself as one of those born with a "nice sense," and he may have had his tastes for fine clothes cultivated by his unnamed professor, though he needed little encouraging.

Back in Richmond, Thompson entered the law offices of James

A. Seddon. He was apparently searching for a profession which would allow him a maximum of social opportunity, and the law seemed adequate. It was also a lucrative profession, and Richmond afforded the most promising practices in Virginia. After two years in Seddon's office, Thompson returned to the University, paid his seventy-dollar fee to law professor Henry St. George Tucker and spent sufficient effort on his classes to graduate as a Bachelor of Law on July 4, 1845.

When he returned to Richmond this time, he found that Seddon was serving a term in Congress. This may be why Thompson decided to set up his own law practice over his father's store at Fourteenth and Main streets. What success he had as a lawyer is not recorded. He continued for at least two years, but law seems to have held little interest for him. Much of his energy and interest was diverted into his social life. His father was prospering, and young Thompson saw no reason to work at his profession.

It was a pleasant time for Thompson, those golden days of youth and peace and promise. Richmond was growing and its citizens becoming more affluent. By 1840 the city's population had exceeded thirty thousand and the future looked good if unexciting. As Thompson described it, "days passed and resembled each other.... Such was the capitol of ante-bellum Virginia, a bowery, flowery, humdrum, hospitable little town, prospering in a *festina lente* sort of way."[14]

His social successes, and there were many, were largely of his own making. His contacts through school and college as well as his law practice served as an entree for, as Richmond viewed it, a foreigner. What he accomplished, once accepted, was largely due to his personal charm and diplomacy. Writing of Thompson at this time of his life, John Esten Cooke commented:

His was the charm and delight of a fascinating raconteur — indeed, I may say that he was one of the very best "Story-tellers" or relators of anecdotes, literary or humorous, that I have ever known. For this he certainly had a distinct gift, and I have listened to him with silent delight. His anecdotes were chiefly humorous — of the character called "good stories" — and there seemed to be no end of them. In private, at suppers, at dinner parties, and everywhere with friends, he abounded with them, putting everybody in a good humor with his sparkling witticisms and the point and finish of his discourse.... He was the charm and delight of the circles — and they were the best — in which he moved.... What delightful company he was in those years! How his smiles, his laughter, his unfailing flow of pleasant chitchat drove away "the blues" if his friends were oppressed by them! Leaning back in his comfortable chair in his office in the Law Building — it was a leather-covered arm chair, and he wrote upon an elegant walnut table with a covering of green cloth — how his eyes sparkled, his ready laugh rang, his soft bright eyes lit up! Reading aloud in his rich sonorous voice — he was, after Thackeray, the most delightful reader I ever listened to — or standing and talking, cigar in mouth with a little of the *petit maitre* air, for he was young and petted by society, he interested you, made you laugh; you forgot the passage of time as you listened, and went away in a good humor with yourself and all the world.... What impressed you most in him was his charming personality, the easy and graceful comingling of the literateur and the man of society. In Paris he would have taken his place, and of right, among the attractions of the literary *salons* and become famous among the wits of the wittiest city in Europe.[15]

Such traits by themselves might have been enough to make him popular, but he was also adept at all kinds of games, "one of the finest whist players in Virginia, and the crack billiard player of Richmond."[16]

While not handsome, he was physically attractive, as Cooke's description of him shows:

He was small in stature and of delicate appearance. His eyes were dark and had a peculiar softness and brightness — the expression varying and reflecting every emotion. He had chestnut hair, curling naturally, wore a very heavy brown beard and mustache, and was extremely nice in his dress and careful of his personal appearance. He was even criticized occasionally as exhibiting a tendency to foppery; but all about him was in the very best taste, and his manners only seemed peculiar perhaps from their instinctive refinement and courtesy which spring from association with ladies and cultivated persons generally, and the pursuit of the *belles lettres* student. In his appearance, bearing, and habits, he was essentially a gentleman of the most refined tastes; and certainly his manner — with the exception of a slight reserve and ceremony at times — was delightful.[17]

Of this man's life up to this point, there is little to suggest the description given by Charles Marshall Graves: "Thompson's personal life was gentle and sad; his literary career a tragedy."[18] Perhaps life was too much of a game. He seems to have plotted his social contacts with the precision of a master chess player, one who perfected every phase of the game. He saw living as an art form, but he had not yet discovered his medium of expression. Marion Harland (pseudonym of Mary Virginia Terhune), who seems to

have resented Thompson for giving an unfavorable review to her
first book, suggested something of his sense of unfulfilment:

He had ambition, and had succeeded in acquiring a sort of world-weary
air, and a gentle languor of tone and bearing which might have been
copied from D'Israeli's *Young Duke,* a book in high favor in his circles. I
never say "Johnny" — as graceless youths who went to school with him
grieved him to the heart by calling him on the street — without thinking of
the novel. Like most caricatures, the likeness was unmistakable.[19]

It is more than likely that Thompson's "world-weariness" in the
years immediately following his degree in law was very much what
it seemed, weariness. He did not like law, nor was he particularly
successful at it; and while his social activities were a passion, they
were not enough to fulfill his "ambition." Within a two-year
period, he had determined to make his way as a writer, but he had
no certain idea of how to go about it. On the basis of vague hopes
and vaguer expectations, he had begun to look for a place on some
magazine. It was with this intention that in September, 1847, he
went to New York for a series of interviews. Quite naturally, his
father had hoped that young Thompson could stay in Richmond.
So it was that, when in September B. B. Minor, editor of the
Southern Literary Messenger, announced his intention to sell the
Messenger and take a teaching position in Staunton, Virginia, the
senior Thompson began negotiations for the purchase of the
magazine. John Reuben had known Minor for some time through
their connection with the Virginia Historical Society. It is possible
that he had written some items for the *Messenger.* From New York
he wrote to Minor:

My father has written to me proposing that I should take the *Messenger*
(on your removal to Staunton) if we could agree upon terms of sale and
other arrangements. I am so situated at present that I cannot immediately
return to Richmond to treat with you on the subject, and I write to request
that you will defer disposing of the magazine until my return which will
not certainly be later than the 24th of the present month. I do not doubt
that if I were at home we could come to an understanding mutually
agreeable and satisfactory and I only ask that you will so far oblige me as
to extend the time of the sale till I can see you in person.[20]

Later that month the twenty-four-year-old lawyer became owner
and editor of the South's most distinguished magazine, for a cost

of twenty-five hundred dollars, provided by his father.

The years that followed acquisition of the *Messenger* were filled for Thompson with his new occupation and with his expanding social life. Now more than ever he attended the city's dinners and elaborate balls, its concerts, performances by famous artists, and state fairs, often serving in some official or honorary function. His offices at the *Messenger* were located at the very hub of activity, socially, politically and commercially. On those days when the work was light, he would gather in his own office or the *Whig*'s — a local newspaper — or in the Richmond Reading and News Room with friends, lawyers, journalists, doctors, business men; here they smoked and discussed politics and matters of local interest. The same group often met again at dinner and continued the talk.

He and Billy Munford often arranged more intimate parties for whist, in particular for Miss Lucy Haxall and Miss Mary Pegram, "and hearts were usually trumps. These two gallants are said to have been ardent in their devotion, but success did not crown their efforts."[21] Whatever his social losses may have been at this time, Thompson seems to have "whistled them down" and gone on to other things — though Miss Lucy Haxall was of continuing interest for at least another decade. He was a very busy man during these years, with the ladies, public affairs, his magazine, and his plans to write an extensive history of English literature. He even tried to keep up his law practice.

Although he was not much involved in politics, he did campaign for the election of his fellow Virginian, Zachary Taylor, the Whig Party candidate for president in 1848. After the successful campaign, the Whig Party turned to the problem of disciplining those members who had refused to support the national candidate. One of these was John Minor Botts, the Congressional representative from Richmond. Young Thompson was a member of the Whig splinter group called the "friends of the Administration," which met to name another candidate to oppose Botts. Led by William H. Macfarland, the group named Mr. Lee. The Whig vote in Richmond was split, and the Democratic nominee, Thompson's former employer, James Seddon, won.

Thompson seems to have taken even less part in politics after this. But he did have clear and firm political beliefs which he defined in a letter to his friend Thomas C. Reynolds of Charleston, South Carolina, shortly after Taylor's inauguration; he wrote, "What you say with regard to General Taylor's Administration does not surprise me, for just in proportion as I am pleased with his course shall I expect you to disapprove it: at such antipodal positions are we in the political world, — you an ultra States Rights Free Trader, I a high Protectionist and Internal Improvement advocate."[22] It is worth noting that here and elsewhere, Thompson did not let his political differences interfere with his friendships. Politics was a minor part of his life at this time. Most of his time was spent with the affairs of the *Southern Literary Messenger.*

The *Messenger* had come into being in August, 1834, the brainchild of Richmond printer Thomas H. White. With the help of James E. Heath and E. V. Sparhawk, White edited the journal, its original purpose being to provide a journal of literary distinction for the South. In March, 1835 the *Messenger* published "Berenice, A Tale" by a brilliant, unknown young writer, who in the next four months published a number of other items, including "Lionizing," "Morella," "Hans Pfall," "Bon Bon," and "The Coliseum." That July the young writer, Edgar Allan Poe, was named editor, and the popularity of the *Messenger* increased greatly. Under Poe the number of *Messenger* subscribers grew from seven hundred to more than three thousand five hundred, but Poe remained only about a year and a half. From 1837 till his death in 1842, White managed the journal himself, though he was greatly aided by another famous Richmonder, Mathew Fontain Maury, "the Pathfinder of the Seas." In 1843 Benjamin B. Minor purchased the rights from the White estate and became owner and editor until he sold, first, all the printing materials to Macfarlane and Fergusson, his printers, and second, in October 1847, his proprietorship as owner and editor to John R. Thompson. Earlier, in 1845, Minor had purchased the rights to William Gilmore Simms's journal, *The Southern and Western Magazine,* published in Charleston. When Thompson became editor, he inherited the cumbersome title of *The Southern and Western Literary Messenger and Review.* With the January issue of 1849, Thompson reverted to the original title.

Since its beginning in White's job-printing office over Anchor's Shoe Store at Fifteenth and Main streets, the *Messenger* had moved twice. From its cramped quarters on Main Street, White moved it to the Museum Building on the southeast corner of Capitol Square, where Franklin Street runs up to it. Here it shared the building with the *Richmond Whig.* When the Museum Building was ordered demolished by the government, Minor, who had taken over ownership by this time, built the Law Building, also in Capitol Square, into which he moved the *Messenger* in January of 1847. The editor's offices were on the second floor; the printing, binding and mailing rooms took up the third and fourth floors. Here the *Messenger* remained throughout Thompson's thirteen-year leadership and then through that of George W. Bagby until it ceased publication in 1864. Throughout its life, William Macfarlane and John W. Fergusson were its principal typesetters and printers. When the first issue was printed in 1834, Macfarlane was White's foreman and Fergusson an apprentice. In 1853 they became joint owners. Thompson continued as their editor till 1860.

In the October 1847, issue, Minor announced the new editorship for the *Messenger* and cited his successor as a man "well endowed by nature, having enjoyed the advantages of the best collegiate education, fond of literature, acquainted with its best authors, accustomed to the use of his pen, and quite enthusiastic in his devotion to the *Messenger*."[23] But Minor may well have had some misgivings about turning over his journal to a twenty-four-year-old, untried editor with no business experience. "What guarantee was there that the magazine, then, as now, one of the first in the Union, would be conducted properly?"[24] asked Dr. Bagby in 1860. There was little need to worry. Whatever he lacked in experience, the young editor made up for in enthusiasm, native ability, and a good understanding of what his readers wanted. His main problem, throughout, was to cultivate readers among the vast majority, North and South, who cared nothing about reading, and to bring those who did to accept a Southern magazine. He found it particularly galling that Southern readers preferred Northern magazines to the *Messenger*. In 1850 he complained to A. L. Taveau of Charleston about the near bankruptcy of the magazine: "while thousands of dollars are spent by Southern men to pay Northern magazines to abuse them."[25] Taveau responded, with understandable bias, that he "would not even spend the 'hours of idleness' in turning the pages of the 'Yellow Cover' trash issued in Philadelphia, yet for which every man, boy and girl, North and South, appear to have such a perfect mania to consume every shilling which they accidently have in their pockets."[26] Doubtless, there is exaggeration in the estimate of the money spent on Northern periodicals, but it is evident that the South did prefer Northern magazines. It was the thing to do.

To win the Southern reader was one of Thompson's major goals, but he wanted also to make the *Messenger* respectable on a national

scale; and so he advised his readers in his first editorial in the
November 1847, issue.

We shall assuredly "contract our powers" in no "pent-up Utica" of
narrow and parochial feeling, but shall recognize the kindlings of genius in
whatever section of the "ONE BROAD LAND" they may be seen and
foster genuine talent wherever it asserts its native dignity and truth.[27]

Put briefly, Thompson had three broad goals for the *Messenger*:
(1) to be national in content and appeal; to be, nevertheless, (2) a
champion of Southern literature; and (3) to be nonpolitical in its
overall attitude. Also implicit in the passage quoted above was the
intention to discover and recognize new talent, a goal in which
Thompson succeded better than in his other, more explicit goals. It
was to be in the discovery of new talent that the national and
regional appeal were made one, for Thompson believed all his life
that the South was on the verge of a great literary awakening, that
the talent to please all the world was waiting in the South to be
nurtured into greatness.

These ideas had already been conveyed to Minor in a letter written before he had made the decision to move to Staunton, and this
attitude may have been a consideration in his decision to sell to
Thompson. Thompson promised that in his hands "while always
prompt to defend Southern interests, it will maintain a strictly
neutral ground. No attempt to array one portion of the Union
against the other or to excite sectional feelings and jealousies will
ever meet with countenance in its pages."[28] This and indeed the
whole job of editing, was a much greater task than Thompson had
expected. Shortly after the purchase, he declared his intention to
continue as a lawyer. "It is not my intention," he told his readers,
"to abandon my profession, but to continue as heretofore a
practiner of the law."[29] But he overestimated his energy; he
probably never again entered the court room as an attorney.

His first task was to establish himself as editor in the minds of
publishers and writers, and he wisely chose to use a very personal
approach to the problem. He was a man who made close and lasting friendships and made them easily. He had an attractive manner
and was genuinely friendly, easy to be with and ingratiating.
Always he reflected good taste, and his integrity was unquestioned.
Among the many great and near-great personalities he met in a life
full of famous people, he was always deemed a friend worth

having. His opinions and abilities were more respected by the great and moral men and women among his acquaintances on both sides of the Atlantic. Doubtless, he was somewhat aware of this ability to "win without wooing" even in 1847, for one of the first things he did after taking over the magazine was to visit New York again. Here he had friends and family connections on his mother's side; but it was primarily to publishers and editors that he addressed his attention. He interviewed as many of his prospective clientele as possible, and between the contacts he reveled in examining new editions as he visited the various New York publishing houses. He was fascinated by numbers, figures, manuscripts, stacks of paper, rows of books; he appreciated the heft of a fat manuscript and the regular beauty of the printed page as well as the artistry of calligraphy, ancient and modern. He wrote for the *Messenger* in January of 1848, "There is to us, in a well arranged and orderly book-store, an attraction, which we make no effort to resist.... We confess a passion for the curious and the odd in books [and]...all the most delicious steel engravings."[30] He was also, all his life, an ardent collector of autographs, autograph manuscripts, and letters of famous men and women.

With publishers he made arrangements for new books to be sent to the *Messenger* for review and for journals to be sent on an exchange basis. He also arranged for correspondents from New York and from Paris and London, in order to gain an international interest for the *Messenger*. W. W. Mann was at this time commissioned to send a series of letters from Paris, and others wrote from other cities of literary events of general importance. Thompson also accepted several articles on English authors and arranged for a flow of articles from Northern writers to the *Messenger*. Within the year he traveled South as far as Charleston, making the same type of contacts, meeting authors and prospective subscribers, visiting William Gilmore Simms at Woodlands.

One of the first Northern writers recruited by Thompson was Richard Henry Stoddard, who was to become Thompson's literary executor. For the June 1849 issue of the *Messenger* Stoddard wrote "The Broken Goblet," a translation from the German. He continued to publish in Thompson's journal as long as the pay was competitive, which it ceased to be in 1851. Park Benjamin, a well-known New York editor, published "Hundred Thousand Clowns" in the December 1848 issue and served after that time as New York correspondent. Other Northern writers who wrote for the

Messenger during Thompson's time include Mrs. L. H. Signourney, H. T. Tuckerman, Henry Wadsworth Longfellow, Matilda Dana, Donald Grant Mitchell (Ik Marvel), Elizabeth Ellet, Mary E. Wells, Sarah H. Whitman, Francis S. Osgood, Thomas Dunn English, Thomas Bailey Aldrich, and some lesser known writers.[31]

The writer most significant among these was "Ik Marvel." Before Thompson discovered him, he had published only one rather unpromising piece. Thompson saw where his real talents lay and encouraged the young author to develop his humorous stories. After two short articles in 1848, "Man Overboard" and "A Ride in the Rain," Ik Marvel firmly established himself as one of America's best humorists with "A Bachelor's Reverie" in 1849. J. M. Legaré wrote to Thompson, expressing a popular opinion, "I consider without exception Ik Marvel's 'Bachelor's Revery' the best magazine article of the day — or more definitely, of the present year — superior to anything to be found, within that period, in either *Blackwoods* or *Knickerbocker,* the only two magazines in our language, of course, with which the *Messenger* may be classed. It is a masterly production of its kind."[32]

In terms of interest and quality the *Messenger* was doing well under its young editor, but it was not doing well financially. Neither were the Thompsons. Sometime between October 1847 and October 1848 the elder Thompson suffered a severe financial setback and was no longer able to support his son's enterprises; he may even have become somewhat dependent on his son. Thompson had no reserve to fall back on and evidently had let his law practice lapse. On October 17, 1848, he wrote Philip Pendleton Cooke, one of his closest friends and supporters:

The best way I could possibly conclude this scrawling epistle would be in writing you a check for the amount of my indebtedness to you, but as I am still in the vocative case with reference to the substantive, *Pecunia,* I must continue still longer to be your debtor, and to draw on your patience instead of my banker. Whatsoever opinions I may have secured "from all sorts of people" about the *Messenger,* it is pretty certain I have had no "golden" ones, so that, with thanks for your kindly forbearance, I must close with no more "valuable consideration" than warmest regards of yours sincerely.[33]

In the following year he commented to another friend, "I have had great trouble and pecuniary embarrassment in its management so far, but hope for better times."[34] John Esten Cooke, Philip's brother, attributed this early money drought to a poor-paying clientel. Many of the Southern subscribers to the *Messenger* were "honest, sober, lovable gentlemen" who used credit almost exclusively.[35] For example, former President John Tyler apologized to Thompson, explaining, "I regret a moment's delay in paying up my arrears to the *Literary Messenger.* We farmers are, however, dependant on our crops and so soon as I can realize the proceeds of recent sales I shall cease to be your debtor."[36] Perhaps Tyler and others did pay their late bills, for the *Messenger* continued. A goodly number of contributors came from the North, particularly in 1850, although Thompson could pay only one or one-and-a-half dollars per page while Northern publications were paying three to five dollars per page.

Already sectional antagonism was exerting itself. Sectional rivalry between North and South was increasingly commercial, literary, and political. Out of the germ of Puritan-vs-cavalier polarity of the earliest settlements in America had grown two antithetical views of life. In the mid-nineteenth century the inbred hostilities were being manifested primarily in the struggle over slavery, a debate which would not be settled until the war was over and the *Messenger* had ceased to be published. More and more, the *Messenger* looked to the South for its support. Partly as a result of the sectional antagonisms, Thompson began to emphasize the development of a Southern literature, not that such a development had ever been in Thompson's mind a subject of secondary importance. In his first letter to the public on the intentions of the *Messenger,* in October 1847, he asked,

Shall the *Messenger* ever want friends in the South, of whose rights it has ever been the peculiar guardian? I cannot believe it. I appeal to the literary intelligence of Virginia, of every state between the Potomac and the waters of the Gulf of Mexico, to sustain and foster it, and I have an abiding trust that this appeal will not be in vain.[37]

In supporting a distinctly Southern literature, Thompson was responding to the most popular desires of men of letters in the South. All of the other leading Southern reviews, including *DeBow's Review, The Southern Quarterly Review* and *Russell's Magazine,* had supported or were actively to encourage writers of the region. In no small part, the South felt an inferiority to the

North, whose leaders of urban industry expressed a longstanding contempt for the rural mentality of the South. The South, at least the reading South, felt at a particular disadvantage in answering the sophisticated arguments of abolitionists such as Lowell and Emerson. The way to counter the intelligentsia of the North was, of course, to develop the intelligentsia in the South. Then, too, in this drive for a Southern literature there was already some stray essence of the idea of separation, of a separate and distinct nation of Southern states, literarily and politically sovereign. Thompson himself did not think in these terms; he valued the Union and argued on its behalf up to the time of Lincoln's call for volunteers. The man among his Southern literary friends who did lead the fight for separation, the man who had created a magazine for that purpose was, of course, William Gilmore Simms.

Simms had for years been working hard to develop a Southern literature. In 1835 he had given support to the *Southern Literary Journal,* which was edited by Daniel K. Whitaker and published in Charleston. This little journal, plagued by sentimental rubbish from the beginning, expired in 1839. He then supported the *Messenger,* when he could afford to, until he started his own journal, *The Southern and Western Magazine,* which he sold to Minor in 1845. After this time he sent to the *Messenger* works which he could probably not place in the better-paying Northern journals. Early in Thompson's tenure as editor, Simms became a regular correspondent of the young editor, urging him to make of the magazine an organ for political statements, a "proper vehicle for the true political opinion of Virginia."[38] Thompson resisted until almost the last moment; but Simms seems never to have resented Thompson's political neutrality. He sent Thompson a number of contributions, including in 1851 and 1852 two dramas, *Norman Maurice* and *Michael Bonham.* All this despite the fact that in 1849 he again was editing a review himself — *The Southern Quarterly Review,* which lasted until 1856. Still, Simms did support the *Messenger* by subscribing to it, advertising it in local papers, and encouraging his friends and acquaintances to buy it. He also remained a lifelong friend and supporter of Thompson.

CHAPTER 2

The Deaths of Two Poets

IN 1849 and 1850, in the space of four months, two of Thompson's literary friends died: Edgar Allan Poe, Thompson's most famous acquaintance up to this time, on October 7, 1848, and Philip Pendleton Cooke, Thompson's dearest friend, on January 20, 1850, at the age of thirty-three. Both deaths were viewed as genuinely tragic events by Thompson, and he lamented the first and grieved over the latter. His comments on Poe's personality and behavior in Richmond have kept Thompson's name before the literary historian as no other event in his life did. The death of Cooke led Thompson to the discovery of a talent and a friendship perhaps even greater than Philip's. This talent belonged to Philip's brother, John Esten Cooke, a writer to whom at least one literary historian, Carl Holliday, as late as 1906 referred, as "Perhaps the most widely known and most popular novelist the South has ever known."[1] Perhaps the friendship that now grew up between Thompson and John Esten Cooke transcended the friendship between Thompson and Philip. The Cooke brothers also had played important roles in the events surrounding Poe's literary and personal reputation.

Poe and Thompson first met in the summer of 1848, toward the end of July, after a stranger had called at Thompson's home and left a message with his mother that a man, calling himself Poe, had for a week or more been at a tavern in the dockside of Richmond, and his friends ought to look after him. Thompson went immediately to look for him, but failing to find him left his card with a tavern keeper, one Jacob Mull. The man, however, had been identified; it was Poe. He had left that day to visit the Mackenzie home, where his sister, Rosalie, lived. Some ten days later, pale and correct, a man he had never seen came to Thompson's office and said, "My name is Poe."[2]

Thompson knew of Poe as Richmond's most famous celebrity at

that time. The *Messenger* owed to Poe, if not its life, at least its reputation as the most distinguished Southern magazine, although Poe had not been on friendly terms with the previous editors. Thompson's sister, Susan P. (Thompson) Quarles, had attended classes in a school at which Rosalie Poe, the poet's sister, taught in 1836. Philip Cooke, at Poe's urging, had started a biography of Poe, and many of the Richmond people Poe had known as a youth, including Robert C. Stanard, Poe's school chum and the son of Poe's "Helen," the Mackenzies, and John H. Pleasants, were friends of Thompson. So he was understandably interested in meeting Poe.

The description given of Poe by Thompson at this time having been the cause of much discussion, in many cases, has caused Thompson to be seen in an unfavorable light. Much of the controversy has to do with two letters in which Thompson described Poe as he appeared in 1848 and 1849. To his friend, Philip Pendleton Cooke, Thompson wrote of Poe as having been "for three weeks horribly drunk, discoursing 'Eureka' to barroom audiences."[3] A year later he was to write to E. H. N. Patterson with equal distaste for Poe's behavior, which evidently disgusted the rather proper young editor. But while he clearly disapproved of Poe's drinking and self-pitying postures, he was quite willing to offer all that he could afford in the way of friendship and support, for he recognized and greatly admired Poe's genius. When Poe first presented himself, Thompson was further impressed with his appearance:

He was unmistakably a gentleman of education and refinement with indescribable marks of genius in his face of marble whiteness. He was dressed with perfect neatness; but one could see signs of poverty in the well-worn clothes, though his manner gave no consciousness of the fact.[4]

Thompson unhesitatingly acceded to his request that Poe might have his mail addressed to the *Messenger.* He also offered Poe the use of a desk in his own office and of a place to sleep in the adjoining room. But Poe preferred to share bachelor quarters with John H. Pleasants, a mutual friend and editor of the Richmond *Whig.* While he stayed there, Thompson urged him to write for the *Messenger,* and Poe turned over to him "The Rationale of Verse," which he had already prepared as a lecture, and a review of the poems of Mrs. Sarah Anne Lewis, Poe's Baltimore friend and benefactor — known as Estelle. But according to Thompson, Poe was not always "lucid" enough to write. Mary E. Phillips wrote of this relationship between Poe and Thompson, incorporating many of Thompson's own words, but the particular significance of her report is the slant of her language, which is a major basis for the unfavorable reputation of Thompson.

Thompson mentioned that he was anxious for Poe to write something "for print, but his 'lucid intervals' were so brief and infrequent it was impossible." The "Rationale of Verse" Thompson took more "as charity"; for though "exhibiting great acquaintance with the subject," it was "too *bizarre* and too technical" for general readers. Thompson's letter concluded with "Poe is a singular fellow." On this letter Mr. Whitty's comments are: "It is not thought that Thompson saw much of Poe on this visit, so this information about him must have been second hand," and Mr. Whitty definitely adds, that Poe was sober enough, at this time, to write many columns of MS., some given away by Thompson — one, "a work of manual art," . . . besides his "Rationale of Verse," a review of Mrs. Lewis's Poems. . . . Truly Poe was a "singular fellow," according to Thompson, to have written so much and so well when "horribly drunk" for those "three weeks," and needed time for his recovery during this Richmond visit. It might be well to bear in mind that none of these *known* Poe MSS. betrays an *unsteady head, or handwriting!*[5]

Much of this material, however, including all of the "Rationale of Verse," was written before Poe came to Richmond, and he was there seven, not three, weeks.

After Poe left Richmond that summer, Thompson wrote him several times.[6] In December Poe answered Thompson's request for contributions to the *Messenger,* regretting that he was too late for the January issue. In January Poe proposed that the *Messenger* reprint the opening chapter of his "Marginalia" — previously published in the *Democratic Review* some years earlier. The chapter appeared in the *Messenger* in April of 1849 with this introduction:

Some years ago Mr. Poe wrote for several of the Northern magazines a series of critical brevities under the title of "Marginalia." They attracted great attention at that time and since, as characteristic of the author, and we are sure that our readers will be gratified at his resuming them in the *Messenger.*[7]

In May, June, July, and September further chapters were published. Poe wrote Thompson at least six times before he returned to Richmond in July. In the *Messenger* office he prepared a review of the poems of Mrs. Frances S. Osgood and the September "Marginalia" chapter.

On August 17 he delivered an address on the "Poetic Principle," which was attended by John Esten Cooke and John M. Daniel, and probably by Thompson. Poe stayed in Richmond until September 27 when he left for Baltimore. On the day before that departure, Poe stopped by the *Messenger* office. Thompson had either lent or advanced him five dollars, and as he left, he turned to Thompson and said, "By the way, you have been very kind to me, — here is a little trifle that may be worth something to you." He handed Thompson a small roll of paper with the verses of "Annabel Lee" written on it.

Poe went from Richmond to Baltimore, and there he died on October 7. The *Richmond Whig* carried a notice of his death and a tribute to him on October 9, and the semi-weekly issue of the same paper reprinted an account of his death and burial from the *Baltimore Patriot*. In New York on October 9 appeared in the *Tribune* the infamous article signed "Ludwig," which included the sentence, "Edgar Allan Poe is dead. He died in Baltimore yesterday. The announcement will startle man, but few will be grieved by it."[8] This notice was written by Poe's literary executor, Rufus W. Griswold. Before the month was out, Griswold wrote to Thompson asking him to do what he could to gather information, material, and manuscripts for the edition of Poe's works he was preparing. The letter said in part,

I heard of the death of Poe one evening at 7 o'clock, and wrote hastily for the next day's Tribune a notice of him, which you may have seen — or an extract of it certainly, in the Home Journal. Poe was no friend of mine, but I knew him well. I think the imperfect and rude sketch of his character, which Willis has copied, is just. I was surprised to learn that he left a written request that I should be his literary executor and editor. It is difficult for me to fulfill the duties this devolves upon me, but I have already commenced printing, and shall very soon — say 3 weeks — have ready two octavos of 500 pages each of his works.... These two volumes will be introduced by a Memoir — (in brief) by J. R. Lowell....[9]

Shortly after this, Thompson was in New York, where he dined with N. P. Willis and met Griswold. These three had many subjects in common, and it is possible that Poe was not mentioned; but it is improbable.[10]

The month following Poe's death, on November 9, Thompson responded to E. H. N. Patterson, a young man with whom Poe had discussed his plans for the *Stylus,* a new magazine which Poe had planned to edit with Patterson's financial backing. The letter has rarely been printed in full:

Your letter making inquires of a personal nature concerning poor Poe has been lying on my table some days. I avail myself of the first leisure moment to reply to it.

My first acquaintance with the deceased was in the spring of 1848, when I accidently learned that a person calling himself Edgar A. Poe had been, for a fortnight, in a debauch, in one of the lowest haunts of vice upon the warves in this City. If you have ever visited Richmond, you may perhaps know that the business portion of the town and the sites occupied by the residences exclusively are distant from shipping by a mile and a half, so that very few persons not actually engaged in commercial affairs ever visit the landing at all. As soon as I heard the name Poe in this connection my worst suspicions were excited, and I at once took a carriage and went to seek him. It was a very warm day in the latter part of May or early in June. When I reached the purlieus of this abandoned quarter, I learned that such a person had indeed been there, drunk, for two weeks, and that he had gone a few hours previous without hat or coat, to the residence of Mr. John MacKenzie. From that time until his death we were much together and in constant correspondence. I did all I could to restrain his excesses and to relieve the pressure of his immediate wants (for he was extremely indigent), but no influence was adequate to keep him from the damnable propensity to drink, and his entire residence in Richmond of late was but a succession of disgraceful follies. He spoke of himself as the victim of pre-ordained damnation, as *l'ame perdue,* a soul lost beyond all hope of redemption. For three weeks previous to his departure from Richmond he had been sober — a Son of Temperance. But no confidence could be placed in him in any relation of life, least of all in antagonism to his fatal weakness. He died, indeed, in delirium from drunkenness; the shadow of infamy beclouded his last moments

> And his soul from out that shadow
> Shall be lifted never more!

But who shall judge harshly of the dead? Mercy benignantly tempers the divine Justice, and to this Justice we commit his spirit.

Poe had spoken to me of your design with reference to the literary enterprise of which you speak. You were fortunate, I think, in not having embarked in it, for a more unreliable person than he could hardly be found. I have not, as yet, recovered his trunk, so that I cannot tell you whether or not he left any unpublished MSS. The day before he went

North from Richmond, I advanced him a small sum of money for a prospective article which he probably never wrote. His complete works will be brought out by the Rev. Dr. Griswold.[11]

Yet in the same month in which he wrote this letter, Thompson published his tribute to Poe in the *Messenger.* After commenting on the many reports that had already been published on Poe's death, Thompson goes on to say,

We feel it due the dead, however, as editor of the magazine which owes its early celebrity to his efforts, that some recognition of his talent, on the part of the *Messenger,* should mingle with the general apotheosis which just now enrolls him on the list of "Heroes of history and gods in song."

Thompson briefly sketches Poe's connection with the *Messenger* and comments on his gifts as an editor, tale-writer, and poet. He writes a sound and impressively durable estimate of Poe as a writer, and also notes that Poe's "tomahawk" style of criticism — of which Thompson generally disapproved — attracted readers and had made the *Messenger* popular:

Those who will turn to the first two volumes of the *Messenger* will be struck with the number and variety of his contributions. On one page may be found some lyric cadences, plaintive and inexpressibly sweet, the earliest vibrations of those cords which have since thrilled with so many wild and wondrous harmonies. On another some strange story of the German school, akin to the most fanciful legends of the Rhine, fascinates and astonishes the reader with the verisimilitude of its improbabilities. But it was in the editorial department of the magazine that his power was most conspicuously displayed. There he appeared as the critic, not always impartial, it may be, in the distributing of his praises, or correct the positions he assumed, but ever merciless to the unlucky author who offended by a dull book.... To the envious obscure, he might not indeed seem entitled to the first literary honors, for he was versed in a more profound learning and skilled in a more lofty minstrelsy, scholar by virtue of a large erudition and poet by transmission of a divine spark....

Unquestionably he was a man of great genius. Among the *literateurs* of his day he stands out distinctly as an original writer and thinker. In nothing did he conform to established custom. Conventionality he condemned. Thus his writings admit to no classification, and yet in his most eccentric vagaries he was always correct. The poems of Mr. Poe are remarkable, above all other characteristics, for the exceeding melody of the versification. *Ulalume* might be cited as a happy instance of this quality.

But here Thompson inserts a remark that is at once unkind — a quality very rare in his criticism — in bad taste, and uncomfortably close to Griswold's comment in the "Ludwig" article: "The untimely death of Mr. Poe occasioned a very general feeling of regret, although little genuine sorrow was called forth by it, out of the narrow circle of his relatives."

Next, Thompson quotes a letter to him from Henry Wadsworth Longfellow, which regretted the death of Poe and included the remark, "The harshness of his criticism I have never attributed to anything but the irritation of a sensitive nature, chafed by an indefinite sense of wrong." Thompson seems to have agreed with the sentiment. He then quotes "Annabel Lee" and concludes:

In what we have said of Mr. Poe, we have been considering only the brighter side of the picture. That he had many and sad infirmities cannot be questioned. Over these we would throw in charity the mantle of forgetfulness. The grave has come between our perception and his errors, and we pass them over in silence. They found indeed a mournful expiation in his alienated friendships and his early death.[12]

Here it seems only fair to judge that Thompson had very little evidence on which to appraise Poe otherwise. His friendship with Poe was never intimate; there was almost no one among his friends and acquaintances who knew Poe and who approved of his conduct or felt any warm friendship with him. Griswold and others in the North who knew Poe had made it clear that he was not their friend, with Willis the exception. Thompson, in short, lived in a society in which public opinion was almost solidly against Poe, and not without some good reasons. Even the women who were so attracted to the moody poet withdrew from him after a while because they found they could not live in a "world of moan." None could know the depth of Poe's pain, but many felt his complaining and histrionic personality was unmanly.

Thompson did seem to understand him better than most of Poe's other friends; and when he urged Poe to work, it was for the good of the writer as well as of the *Messenger*. Still, Thompson clearly and honestly felt that Poe had wasted a great gift, and he faced the dilemma of the moral man: how to condemn actions and attitudes, which are inevitably enmeshed with personality, and not hate the person. He might have ignored Poe's infirmities altogether and spoken of his art only, but once the "Ludwig" article had appeared no commentator on Poe at this time could afford to do so. He could not have held his audience in the folksy, gossipy, little literary world of the United States in mid-nineteenth century. Part of his audience would have assumed that he either did not consider Poe's weaknesses as such or that he was intentionally covering up. The charges against the poet and countercharges published in almost every newspaper and literary journal in America had become exceedingly hostile and created great interest. Thompson, here as so often in his life, tried to bring about a reconciliation by setting an example.

Then came the new edition of Poe's works with the notices of his life by Nathaniel P. Willis and James Russell Lowell, the whole of which was edited by Griswold. Thompson did not review these volumes except for a short note in the February issue of the *Messenger* in which he expressed disappointment. His failure to write a more extensive review was due to limited time; he was out of the town on a visit to New York and Washington for the two weeks immediately preceding the dateline for the March issue. He had done most of the work for that issue, but for the remaining editorial work he appointed John Esten Cooke as interim editor. The one major item yet to be done was the review of the Griswold edition of Poe. Thompson turned this chore over to the fire-eating editor of the *Richmond Examiner,* John Moncure Daniel, whose paper had received review copies of the new volumes.

In Daniel's capable, if somewhat calloused, hands the article grew into a glowing example of what Thompson called the tomahawk style of criticism. It was written, printed, and proofread before Thompson returned. The article was a scathing attack on Poe, during which Daniel added to the other charges the unsupported claim that Poe had attacked his foster father's second wife, Louisa Gabriella Allan. But for their failure to write new essays and for the shabby nature of the edition, Daniel turned with withering scorn on Willis, Lowell, and Griswold, whom he mistakenly assumed to be joint editors. These three, asserted Daniel,

... felt quite pitifully sentimental at his dog's death; and with the utmost condescension they hearkened to the clink of the publisher's silver, and agreed to erect a monument to the deceased genius, in the shape of Memoir and Essay preliminary to his works: Their kindness and their generosity has [sic.] been published to the world in every newspaper. . . . Here it is, at last — and duty compels us to say that this is the rawest, the boldest, the most offensive, and the most [im]prudent humbug that has ever been palmed upon an unsuspecting moon-calf of a world. These three men...have practiced in the publication as complete a swindle on the purcheser as ever sent a knave to the State prison.[13]

When Thompson returned from Washington, the March issue was ready to go to press. He quickly read over the material before releasing it to the printers and decided to let the article be published as it stood. In an editorial note, however, he added a disclaimer, saying that he had nothing to do with the writing of the article.

On the second of April 1850, he wrote Griswold a more detailed apology which he sent by the elder Thompson, who was going to New York on business. He explained to Griswold,

I can scarcely express the mortification I felt, upon my return, at finding in the sheets of the forthcoming number of the *Messenger* the coarse abuse of yourself and Willis, which disfigured the article on Poe. At first I ordered it suppressed, at any expense, but being informed that it would delay the number most unreasonably, I was compelled to send it forth with my personal disclaimer by way of *ammende honorable*. I had indeed given the writer a *carte blanche* to say what he pleased, but I had not the faintest conception that this freedom whould have been abused by attacks upon my esteemed friends. I am sure you did me justice, before reading the Editorial Note, to suppose that I had no hand in the preparation of such vulgar and unmerited strictures.[14]

Joseph Miller seems to think that Thompson allowed the offensive article to stand as revenge on Griswold, who had failed to print Thompson's poetry in his recent anthology. But as nothing else in Thompson's life suggests that he would have been so petty, this does not seem a justified assumption. The correspondence between the two editors seems always to have been very equal in treatment; each asked the other for favors; each offered apologies at times, and, most importantly, each seems quite independently to have believed that Poe was a man of great genius who had some very offensive traits of character. Clearly Thompson had great admiration for Griswold. In October 1850, he wrote in defense of the literary executor's third volume of Poe's works, *The Literati,* which included Griswold's lengthy biography of Poe,

As far as we are capable of judging (and we had some intercourse with Poe at one period of his life), the record is truthful, and while the biographer has been compelled to speak some hard things of this subject, they seem to have been brought out only because their suppression would have been as papable a departure from an honest estimate of the poet, as a direct misstatement of any of his qualities. Kindness to the dead, indeed, requires that we should deal tenderly with their reputations, but there are some cases in which too great fastidiousness would be positive injustice to the living, and this is one of them.[15]

Several critics have supposed Thompson to have known Poe well, which has proved to be unfortunate since they also assume that any error on Thompson's part was intentional. C. M. Graves, for example, states, "Thompson doubtless understood Poe far better than many of his time."[16] This is a misleading statement though it contains some truth. Thompson was certainly better for Poe than most of his other friends in Richmond, for he forced the poet to healthy work, kept him away from liquor, and helped him in money matters when he could. What he knew of Poe, however, was limited to three or four weeks in the summer of 1848 and three months in the summer of 1849. He knew him further by reputation, through mutual acquaintances, through his writings and his letters. Thompson did not presume much beyond that limited knowledge, though he had been accused of doing so.

Much of the misunderstanding of Thompson's relationship with Poe may be traced to Thompson's support of Griswold, which began when, shortly after Poe's death, Griswold wrote Thompson asking for help in gathering information. But Griswold did not at this time or any other ask for Thompson's opinion of Poe or for collaboration. Still, from that time on, Thompson was identified as one of the defenders of Griswold; consequently, he has been discredited in most of his statements on Poe, though Thompson's most damaging statements were in private letters written before the controversy had become so heated, and before he had met Griswold.

Most of those who have written of Thompson have been Poe scholars to whom Thompson was of merely secondary interest; one exception to this rule is Joseph R. Miller, who attacks Thompson's conduct on a number of points. He thinks that Thompson overstated his friendly relations with Poe in his letter to E. H. N. Patterson, stating, "His association evidently was not as intimate as Thompson's letter to E. H. N. Patterson...would indicate." The first writer to point this out, seems to have been John H. Whitty. Mary E. Phillips in her two-volume study of Poe, *Edgar Allen Poe: The Man,* found Whitty's explanation useful and so did Hervey Allen.[17] The passage from which the charge is derived is,

"From that time [the summer of 1848] until his death we were much together and in constant correspondence."[18] Given the facts of Poe's correspondence with Thompson, not all of which has been discovered, the material from Poe published in the *Messenger,* and the time he spent in Richmond, much of it at the *Messenger* office, it does not seem that Thompson overstated the case at all. Obviously, the need to discredit Thompson's testimony has more to do with the other statements Thompson made about Poe, about the time spent in Richmond and his drinking; and, of course, it was part of a larger effort to discredit Griswold.

A little further on Miller regrets that "Thompson did not take up the cudgels in defense of his fellow-townsman...but it must be remembered that the set with which he associated felt Poe had turned his back on his benefactors and had revealed himself a renegade."[19] Yet the set with which Thompson associated included Mr. and Mrs. Robert C. Stanard, the Mackenzies, and most of the other Richmond friends of Poe.[20] It might be also argued, equally well, that Thompson is to be congratulated for resisting support of a man on the basis of state and city pride. On the other hand, Thompson did respect the opinions of the men of his profession in Richmond, and he held a high regard for the sacred nature of the social contract; when an individual violated the order of society, he sinned, unless he served a higher law. The self-serving of the individual genius might be such a higher law, yet it might be just self-serving.

Finally, Miller argues that Thompson criticized Poe and supported Griswold because "Thompson was aspiring to gain a position for his magazine and himself, and consequently catered to the New York editor." This in turn, led him to allow Daniel's attack on Griswold to be published in the *Messenger* as an act of vengeance when Griswold failed to print Thompson's poetry, and then to write begging forgiveness in a manner "fawning," "obsequious," and dishonest. This last term, "dishonest," is deduced from a later statement in which Miller credits Thompson with, at last, having "made an *honest* and successful effort to present accurately...the genius and character of his fellow poet."[21] [My emphasis] There are at least two distinct and perhaps separate incidents here. The group of letters to Griswold which betray so "fawning" a spirit is best represented by the one in which Thompson first apologizes to Griswold for not sending him the background material on Poe and for the scanty pieces he now sends with the letter — an enclosure of two letters from Philip Cooke to Poe and a short statement about Poe's connection with the Allans. Thompson then turns to his own problems:

I see the new edition of the Poets does not give me lines. Well, n'import. As I said to you in making the request (perhaps an indelicate one) for their insertion, I do not think I have any right to a place among our poets, and I think that you have acted with commendable independence to exclude me. I did desire to see the poem the "Greek Slave" in some collection for preservation, but as it does not come up to the standard for your imprinters, I am glad that it has been left out. Pray pardon me, my Dear sir, for troubling you upon so frivolous a subject and think no more of me as a verse maker, but only as your very faithful friend and servant.[22]

The final phrase seems to be merely the conventional obsequiousness of the times that one finds before the signatures of polite letters. In the body of the letter there is certainly a self-conscious effort to be polite in the face of injured vanity; certainly, too, it is ornate in its forced politeness. But Thompson was normally a courteous person in his letters — as in his conduct; whether it is "fawning" and betrays a mean spirit remains a matter of interpretation. I do not find it so.

The other part of the Griswold connection is the review of the first two volumes of the new edition of Poe. The reader is invited now to eavesdrop on an imagined scene in the office of the *Southern Literary Messenger.* Seated together are John Esten Cooke and John R. Thompson, commiserating perhaps over the recent death of Philip Pendleton Cooke; into their company breathing fire enter, John M. Daniel.

Daniel: Well, here it is at last, Griswold's edition. Have you seen it?
Thompson: No, those New York publishers just aren't sending me review books nowadays, and how can I review it if I don't have the book? Would you lend me yours?
Daniel: I'll do better than that, I'll write a review myself for you, and I'm really going to burn some tailfeathers. Do you know what Willis did? Instead of writing a new memoir on Poe's life, he reprinted the "Ludwig" article and then slopped together a couple of more pages and let it go at that. Lowell didn't even do that much. He just reprinted that notice he had written five years ago.
Thompson: Well, you know, I can't be associated with anything that would be critical of my Yankee friends.
Cooke: I'll tell you what, J. R., why don't you take a little vacation and

while you're gone I'll edit the *Messenger*, and Daniel can write the review for me. Maybe you can get back just in time to add a little disclaimer in an editor's note.

Improbable as it may seem, this little dialogue, or something like it is what Miller would have us believe took place. It is far more likely that Thompson did just as he said: he gave Daniel *carte blanche*, knowing that Daniel would probably criticize the editing, the weak and skimpy essay by Willis, and the reprint of Lowell's sketch; and the criticism of Poe might also have been expected to some extent. But it was the "vulgar and unmerited strictures" against Willis, Griswold, and Poe that Thompson did not approve. It is to be noted that Thompson did not apologize for the attack on Lowell; he felt Lowell deserved it and said so. Two other points are worth noting. If Thompson had been fawningly courting Griswold's favor, it is not likely he would have regretted Daniel's abuse of "poor Poe," as he did in his letter, knowing the hostility that Griswold held against Poe. It is also improbable that Daniel would have made the mistake he did, about Willis and Lowell being joint editors, if he had talked about the edition with Thompson, who knew that Griswold was the only editor. Finally, Thompson never criticized Poe's character in any specific detail in print. Publicly he regretted the "infirmities of character" which he could hardly ignore after the public debate between the Griswold faction and the Poe faction, and he always argued that writers should be respectful of the dead. It was only in the letter to Patterson, who had asked to know the worst of his pending association with Poe, that Thompson was openly critical of the dead Poe; and this was not published until many years after Thompson's death.[23] Here, while the criticism is severe, it is not unjustified nor untruthful as far as Thompson was able to judge, nor, except for the confusion over dates, is it inaccurate.

Another mark on Thompson's character has grown out of the letter he wrote Philip Pendleton Cooke, October 17, 1848, after Poe's visit, when Thompson first met him. Here Thompson stated that Poe had left Richmond, probably on September 10 or 11, after having been three weeks "horribly drunk" and after having declaimed "Eureka" in the barrooms. Hervey Allen, following John H. Whitty and Mary E. Phillips, says, "Thompson's description of Poe's doings in Richmond at this time are thought on good authority [Whitty's] to be exaggerated,"[24] and further on he echoes

Whitty and Phillips again: "J. R. Thompson aparently did not see as much of Poe on this visit as some of his later remarks would seem to indicate." Since Allen does not cite which remarks of Thompson's he has in mind in the latter quotation, it is hard to comment on this casual statement which, nevertheless, has the effect of suggesting that Thompson was not a reliable witness. But if we may take the statement made in the letter to Patterson as representative of Thompson's exaggerations ("From this time until his death we were much together and in constant correspondence....") then the evidence of letters and manuscripts and such statements as Allen's own, ("Most of his [Poe's] time, however, was spent on newspaper haunts. He made the office of the *Messenger* his headquarters....") all suggest that Thompson was not exaggerating.[25]

Some inaccuracies in Thompson's letters are undeniable. He says in his letter to Cooke that Poe had been in Richmond three weeks, but it was almost certainly closer to seven. He reported to Patterson in 1849 that Poe had come to the *Messenger* office the day after Thompson had left his card with a local tavern keeper, but in his description of the same event ten years later, he wrote that it was "some ten days later." His statement that Poe was "horribly drunk and discoursing 'Eureka' *every night* to the audiences of Bar Rooms" also is probably exaggerated. Some partial explanation is still possible which does not make out Thompson to be as prejudiced as other, previous, partial explanations.

Thompson's reference to Poe's having remained in Richmond "about three weeks" probably referred to the time after Poe had introduced himself to Thompson. This would still have left about four weeks for Poe to have been in Richmond, even for him to have been "two weeks" in the lower section of town before Thompson heard of him, then ten days before Poe came to the office: a total of about seven and a half weeks. Still, when he wrote Cooke, Poe was still alive, and Thompson had no reason to make statements for effect nor for posterity. His paragraph on Poe is a short one in a long letter; in all fairness it seems reasonable to judge that he did not bother to check his dates and wrote somewhat irritably of his disappointment with Poe. But, of course, Thompson must have been wrong, in his letter to Patterson, about its having been "late May or early June" when he went to look for Poe. It was late July or early August. He was probably wrong, too, about Poe's coming to his office "the next day"; in later years he checked his dates more carefully and noted the ten-day period, which is more than likely correct.

There seems, in particular, a need among several of the Poe scholars to doubt Thompson's assertion that Poe had been "horribly drunk." As late a critic as Edward C. Wagenknecht has perpetuated the doubt. In his *Edgar Allan Poe: the Man behind the Mask* he states:

> We can hear anything we like about Poe's drinking, but the one thing we can be sure of is that he was not a tavern roister; he had neither the virtues nor the vices which flourish in the tavern atmosphere....
> The few stories of pub crawling that have connected themselves with Poe's name rest upon very shaky foundations: thus John R. Thompson reported in October 1848 that Poe had been found in Richmond "horribly drunk, and discoursing *Eureka* to the audiences of Bar Rooms," but this is the same Thompson who calmly records having seen Poe drain a full tumbler of brandy on top of thirteen mint juleps before breakfast, and such a man can hardly be called a creditable witness.[26]

Let us be clear, however, on the fact that Thompson never called Poe a tavern roisterer, and that Thompson did not claim that Poe was drunk when he was declaiming "Eureka" and that Poe did recite "Eureka" in at least one barroom is supported by other testimony than Thompson's.[27] Wagenknecht does not reveal the source of his Thompson story, and the footnote to the passage refers the reader to Arthur Hobson Quinn's *Poe: A Critical Biography,* which makes no mention at all of Thompson's saying anything about Poe's drinking before breakfast. But Quinn does express the ultimate doubt about Thompson's reliability as a witness, for he goes so far as to doubt that Poe went to Richmond at all in 1848, preferring, because he is "irritated" by the "romantic" nature of the tales told about the 1848 visit, a statement from a letter written in 1859 by Mrs. Clemm to the effect that Poe did not visit Richmond from 1837 to 1849. Yet this letter was written to Mrs. Whitman, who had written to Poe in Richmond in 1848. Quinn does, however, admit the possibility. "We shall, of course," he grudgingly concedes, "accept Poe's own testimony in this case, but the visit must have been a minor episode."[28] According to Hervey Allen, however, Poe arrived in Richmond on July 19 and left probably September 10 or 11, about seven and a half weeks.

So justice has been done. If Thompson exaggerated his stories of Poe in his letters, his punishment has fit the crime, for those who have written of him have exaggerated his faults in turn.

Allow me now to jump ahead by a decade, to 1859. In this year Thompson wrote a lecture that he presented, upon request, for years thereafter, but that was lost after his death and not printed until 1929. It is titled "The Genius and Character of Edgar Allan Poe." Its purpose, ostensibly, was "the sincere desire of arriving at a juster estimate of the genius and character of...Poe, albeit with an unaffected distrust of being able to treat fully and fairly so difficult a subject."[29] It was a response to the prejudice and distortion which had colored Poe's name since 1849. And it is probably at this time, with the aid of Mrs. Sarah Helen Whitman and others, that Poe's reputation began its recovery to respectability. Of course, to the Victorian mentality that believed "no good could come from an evil man" and that anyone who was immoral or intemperate in one walk of life was not to be trusted in any other, no reputation, once tarnished, was ever wholly to be redeemed.

Thompson begins his lecture with the recognition that Poe was a complex and manysided person:

There were several Poes at work simultaneously, but apart from each other, all the while that the Poe of flesh and blood was keeping up an unequal fight with poverty whose stronger ally was drink: — there was Poe the critic, a wild man with a tomahawk and a scalping knife, greatly dreaded by the young authors... — there was Poe the romancer, we had almost said the necromancer, forever wandering about in "a wild, wierd clime, out of space out of time" and narrating wonderful accounts of abnormal creatures and supernatural phenomena with so much vraisemblance that hundreds believed him as implicitly as we believe "Livingstone" and "Dr. Kane" — there was Poe the poet, with his singing robes about him, and flinging out notes of wondrous sweetness burdened with an inarticulate human woe, as if "the angel Israfel, whose heart-strings are a lute" had come down to sing on this earth, the valley of bleeding and broken hearts in which we live — there was Edgar Allan Poe, known to the tailors and innkeepers of New York, Philadelphia, and Richmond as a somewhat impecunious individual, given to neglect of bills and sleeping in the markethouse, and others in those cities as a man of seedy and yet respectable appearance, his countenance "sickled o'er with pale cast of thought," his coat threadbare but well brushed, the most polite of "poor gentlemen" — the most easy, opulent and suggestive conversationalist of his age and country.[30]

Of Poe the critic, he wrote:

No man of one-half Poe's keenness and severity has, since his death, sat in judgment upon authorship in America. . . . As a critic in the same sense that Jeffrey and Macauley were critics, Poe was not however entitled to the highest rank. Wonderfully acute and analytical, he saw at once through the whole mechanism of a poem, a story, a scientific treatise or a philosophical discourse, and seized upon the halting measures, false rhymes and stolen passages of the poet, the novelist, and the inaccurate deductions and untenable positions of the writer on physics or political economy, and exposed them with remarkable clearness and precision. His powers of analysis and synthesis were almost equally wonderful.[31]

As a weaver of tales, Thompson wrote of him:

Poe was undeniably the most original and marvelous narrator that has ever enriched English literature with his creations. . . . The supernatural in fictitious composition found in him an interpreter such as it never had before.[32]

Thompson attributed much of the success of Poe's poetry "to the charm of versification":

He was the Beethoven of language, combining it with marvelous skill to exercise a witchery over the readers, and the music of his stanza a "Spirit of Waltz" to which his embodied ideas kept time.[33]

Some of his statements on Poe are clearly and effectively aimed at Griswold's charges as well as those of Daniel. Thompson writes, for example, "Poe was not without capacity of loving tenderly and deeply, and his affection for his wife, his watchful solicitude for her in illness and his poignant anguish at her death, abundantly prove that he did love with a holy and unselfish passion. . . ." [p. 29], and later, "with all his faults, envy, that most despicable trait of the literary pretender, was no part of his nature." [p. 42]. His defense against the charges of plagiarism is particularly original and fair. Of what he calls "an unquestionable plagiarism" in "The Raven," he responds, "The assurance I feel that it is not an accidental imitation detracts in no degree from my admiration of 'The Raven.' If a diamond of wonderous size had crystallized around a pearl, supposing such a thing to be possible in mineralogy, the superior gem would lose nothing of its value thereby, and 'The Raven' surpasses the poem whose beauties it has borrowed as the Koh-i-noor outshines the most exquisite jewel that ever slept in the bosom of the Indian Sea." [p. 33]

His understanding of Poe's psychological personality is another perceptive element of this essay. In Poe's vitriolic criticism, Thompson found self-accusation; "Poe kept on exchanging hard blows with others that he might not turn upon his own consciousness." [p. 51] These feelings of self-reproach were seen as the major weakness in Poe's critical approach: "In Poe's critical writings, therefore, there is an incompleteness, a fragmentary and unsatisfactory treatment of the subject which prevents their being classed among the highest efforts in this department of literature. . . . He was sometimes the mere creature of personal feelings." [p. 14] Such feelings also provided an explanation of Poe's failures in belletristic works as well: "A book healthy and happy throughout, Poe never could have written, for his intellect was not healthy and the man himself was not happy. . . ." He adds, "It is painful to think that he arrived at this eminence by strange and subtle processes of suffering, and that the favorite study of his life was a sort of Frankenstein which held him in the direst subjection." [p. 18]

Finally, of Poe the man Thompson wrote in the light of experience and all that had been said in the previous ten years:

It has always seemed to me that the case of Poe called for the exercise of a larger and more liberal charity than is ordinarily extended to the infirmities of genius. For while he moved about this planet, struggled, suffered, aspired here, owned an American citizenship and was set down in the New York Directory as "Poe, Edgar A., editor, house Fordham," he was at the same time an inhabitant of that shadowy realm of ideas in which the scene of his story was laid and where the music of his verses were borne on the wind. And it was the dreamy abstraction of his character, the indifference he ever manifested for the substantial objects that surround us, which involved him in such a multiplicity of vexations and troubles. . . . I love to think of him as he appeared during the two months which immediately preceded his death, a quiet, easy, seemingly contented and well-bred gentleman, conversing for hours with an opulence of language and of thought that was his alone, projecting new enterprises into literature, and now and then reading aloud some favorite verses of Tennyson and of Longfellow with an inflection and an emphasis that made the exercises as delightful as a sonata of Mozart.[35]

Here, years later, Thompson wrote, "it has always seemed to me," that Poe's case "called for the exercise of a larger and more liberal charity," than it received. In light of all the evidence now available it seems that Thompson's case also deserves, not charity, but honesty.

CHAPTER 3

The Southern Literary Messenger

A S editor of *The Southern Literary Messenger,* Thompson did a number of things well. In addition to remaining in contact with the best writers of his time, in person and by letter, he was from the beginning an astute observer and critic of writers, inexperienced and experienced. As a critic, he was almost the opposite of Poe, being generous and supportive. He pointed out faults where he found them, but his tastes ran to more sentimental expressions than Poe would have tolerated and which few but the very young would admire today. He gave advice as few editors did and was helpful when he could be. He admired the Northern writers quite as much as those from the South, but was seldom, if ever, awed by a great reputation. A fair example of his reviews is taken from the January 1848, *Messenger.* In a notice of the third edition of Long-fellow's *Evangeline,* Thompson comments on the poem, finding it largely praiseworthy. But he begins with a verse parody.

This is another new poem, published by Ticknor of Boston,
Prompted by Longfellow's muse and crowded with exquisite fancies,
Such as we read in "The Voice of the Night" and in "Belfry of Bruges."
Pleasantly told is the tale, and Evangeline, fairest of maidens
Wins, with her tranquil affections a way to the heart of the reader.
Proud though we are of the poet and his old language majestic,
Never should visions so fair be writ in hexameter verses.

Then he mildly chides Longfellow for an inappropriate metaphor.

"Sweet was her breath as the breath of kine that feed in meadows...."
O, Mr. Longfellow! was ever maiden of Arcadie so libelled before![1]

It was with the inexperienced writers that Thompson enjoyed his greatest successes. Longfellow was not likely to learn much from a critic like Thompson, but young writers had a great deal to learn from his acute sense of reality and artistic expression, his humor and gentle guidance. Most of all, Thompson offered an opportunity to have their first, faulty works published in a magazine of national distinction.

Philip Pendleton Cooke hardly falls into the category of an unpublished young writer. When he first published in the *Messenger* in 1848, he was already thirty-one; but certainly Thompson's encouragement and friendship meant much to him nevertheless. He published in every issue of the *Messenger* — except for the August 1848, issue[2] — from the time his essay on Poe first appeared until his death in January 1850. With the death of Cooke, the friendship between Thompson and John Esten Cooke became stronger. John Esten Cooke did not wish to become a professional writer, but he had published a poem in the *Messenger* as early as November 1848. By 1850, when poor health forced Thompson to take a brief vacation just before the March issue of the magazine was due, his faith in young Cooke's ability was so great that he turned the final preparation of the issue over to him. Later in 1854, Thompson urged Cooke on MacFarlane and Fergusson as interim editor for the whole year that Thompson was out of the country. On both occasions Cooke performed his duties with skill and competence. At the same time that he edited the *Messenger,* he also published his most successful novel, *The Virginia Comedians.*

Another young Virginian whose works appeared in the *Messenger* in these early days was James Barron Hope, who at twenty-five published "A Fragment from the Journal of the Late Henry Ellen." Over the next few years he was to publish many items in the *Messenger;* when in 1857 he published his first book of poetry, Thompson reviewed it:

Of Hope's smaller poems it must be said that they are quite unequal, some being hardly worthy of reproduction in his volume, while others are so intense, so truthful, so stirring, so passionate, so tender in their humanity and so magnificent in their lyric swell, that we do not know how to speak of them without subjecting ourselves to the charge of partial extravagance.[3]

In that same year, Thompson recommended that Hope be selected as the poet of the celebration of the two hundred fiftieth anniversary of the settlement of Jamestown. Because of his success at

Jamestown, and on the basis of other patriotic poems, Hope gradually acquired the honorary title of "Virginia's Laureate."

Also encouraged by Thompson was Mrs. Margaret Junkin Preston, the wife of a professor at Virginia Military Institute and daughter of Dr. George Junkin, Lee's predecessor as president of Washington College (later Washington and Lee). Her first contribution, "Apostrophe to Niagera," appeared in August, 1849, followed by many more over the life of the *Messenger*. The support and understanding given Mrs. Preston led to a friendship that lasted beyond the end of Thompson's life. Upon his death she wrote a touching tribute in her poem "The Poet's Grave," and it was to her that another of Thompson's protegées, Paul Hamilton Hayne, wrote after hearing of Thompson's death:

How vividly I recall his appearance! Just 26 years old, slightly but elegantly formed, with a manner far quicker and more vivacious, than it was in after life, — dressed in the height of the prevailing mode, with light-twilled pantaloons, and a blue coat, brass-buttoned, — he shown upon us "Hobbledehoys —" a somewhat radient vision of a man, partly literateur, and partly dandy! We liked him none the less, however, for his touch of the petite maitre — and from that spring morning in the month of May 1849 — when his acquaintance was made — until the end of T's career — I, at least, can affirm that our friendship continued uninterrupted, growing warmer, despite many a year of separation, for our correspondence was never wholly broken off, until within a few months of his decease![4]

To Hayne and his fellow townsman Henry Timrod, who had some of their earliest works published in the *Messenger,* Thompson felt considerable obligation for the amount of quality material they contributed to the journal. Hayne appeared first in the *Messenger* with a short poem, "The Strangers," in the December issue of 1848. His output up to this point had been slight, but the encouragement from Thompson was highly effective and fairly launched Hayne's career. Eight poems appeared in a year's time. Henry Timrod had his start with the *Messenger* the following year under the pen name "Aglaus." And, of course, he too stood at the beginning of a fine career.

Another young lawyer, and Charlestonian, who became at this time a contributor to the *Messenger* was Augustin Louis Taveau, who wrote under the sobriquet of "Alton." He exchanged many letters with Thompson between 1848 and 1856, and the correspondence is a good example of the careful criticism and supportive friendship which Thompson employed with a number of young, uncertain poets who matured under the mentorship of the young editor.

An impressive number of young and not so young aspiring writers were thus nourished and guided by Thompson, though too many to name here. Among those whose names have found some permanent place in the history of Southern literature at least, we might mention Frank Stockton, Susan Talley, William Gordon McCabe, Mary E. Bryan, W. C. Richardson from Alabama, Joseph G. Baldwin, author of *Flush Times of Alabama and Mississippi,* George Washington Harris, and Dr. George W. Bagby. This list will suffice to illustrate that Thompson was an effective developer of new talent, of writers who were most important in making the *Messenger* the voice of the South (which Thompson had held as one of his original goals for the *Messenger*).

His goal of keeping the *Messenger* nonpolitical was not so easily won. Of course, it should be understood that Thompson's intention was primarily to avoid making the *Messenger* a mouthpiece for political parties, i.e. the Whigs and the Democrats. The subjects of slavery and states rights were not always viewed as political matters; but, recognizing their political implication, Thompson generally resisted the temptation, particularly urged by William Gilmore Simms, to make the journal a voice for Southern opinion. Thompson did allow for a loophole in his antipolitical intentions for the *Messenger,* however, for in the original statement of his goals for the magazine in November 1847, he had said, "But as the prefix of Southern to the name of the *Messenger* has always had a particular significance in pointing it out as the guardian of Southern rights and interests, we shall ever be prompt to defend these rights and interests, when they are made the object of ruthless assault. To this extent it will be political and no further."[5]

So it was that when in 1848 James Russel Lowell's *Thoughts on Slavery* was presented to the *Messenger* for review, Thompson argued the Southern point of view. He wrote that he did not think of slavery as a political question, but rather as a part of a way of life and, as such, worthy of the support of those who had a right in a free nation to live as they pleased. His views on slavery were presented in terms which were considered decidedly liberal by Southern standards. He granted that "slavery in its inception is wrong," that "it is detrimental to the interests of the community where it exists," that the government's prohibition of the slave trade was praiseworthy, and that the Colonization Society deserved credit; yet he maintained that "the duty of abolishing this institution does not necessarily follow from the premises." He went on to list the advantages of slavery: (1) "it is vitally connected with every fibre of our social system, (2) the condition of the slave population of itself furnished a strong argument against precipitate change," and (3) slavery was a part of states' rights: "Whatever may be proper and necessary for us to do, whether we are bound by the laws of morals to apply a remedy at all — if so, what remedy shall be — are problems, the solution to which rests exclusively with ourselves. Nor have the confederate States, or the people thereof, any more right, whether with arms or moral means, to compel us to this task, than they would have to assume a similar control over the domestic policy of any nation in Europe."[6]

A majority of Southerners, perhaps even a majority of Virginians, would have considered Thompson's position unacceptably antislavery, and antistates' rights, but Thompson's thinking went even further to the left, for he did not consider the South a separate nation, and against the rising tide of separatism. He struggled, pleaded and urged compromise: "We insist upon the principles of this all-important compromise, we believe its preservation of vital consequence to the stability and integrity of the Union — as we believe the continuance of the Union indispensable to the peace, the prosperity, the strength, and the true glory, of the States which compose it."[7]

A statement rare in the periodicals of its time, North or South for its clearsightedness and lucid reasoning, it managed — while satisfying few — to keep the *Messenger* relatively apolitical at a time when most of its contemporaries were decidedly partisan. Thompson wanted to keep the *Messenger* literary and he believed "faction [to be] eminently pernicious to the graces of literature."[8]

Up to 1854, there had appeared in the *Messenger* only three articles of any importance dealing with slavery. But the Nebraska Bill of 1854 caused great debate, and its popularity as a subject for discussion and the ever sagging finances of the magazine combined to force Thompson to accept many more articles on the subject of slavery than he had been in the habit of doing. Two years earlier another object of heated controversy had led Thompson with his usual restraint, polish, good manners, and reluctance to castigate either author or work to part with his usual avoidance of political subjects. This was, of course, the appearance of the celebrated novel of 1852, Harriet Beecher Stowe's *Uncle Tom's Cabin*. Publication of the work which brought forth thousands of protests from the South, produced another controversy which pushed Thompson farther and farther to the right. In response to the charges of inaccuracy and slander — which still have some currency a hundred and more years later — as well as to further the causes of abolition, Mrs. Stowe compiled a long and copiously documented rebuttal, titled *The Key to Uncle Tom's Cabin*. This work was written in response to her detractors in general, but in particular, Stowe was responding to "a much valued correspondent. . . writing from Richmond, Virginia, "who had sent her a copy, with arguments, of John R. Thompson's "slashing" review of her novel, which had appeared in the pages of the *Messenger*. Of course, slavery had now become a literary matter, and Thompson had not the slightest hesitation about reviewing it in the *Messenger*, but he was not in the habit of writing in the slashing style he now deemed necessary. He first turned to John M. Daniel, who was too busy with the presidential campaign of 1852 to write for the *Messenger*. Then he wrote asking George Frederick Holmes, scholar, educator, critic and author of numerous textbooks, and later (1857) professor of history and literature at the University of Virginia:

I am very sure you think as ill of the book (as an adominable tissue of falsehood and impurity) as Daniel and I do, and there is no doubt whatever that if anybody can use the language as a whip of Scorpions, that man is yourself. I would have the review as hot as hell-fire, blasting and searing the reputation of the vile wretch in petticoats who could write such a volume — I would have it burn like a stick of lunar caustic into the conscience of every really sincere abolitionist who has been deluded by such base misrepresentations of Slavery and the Southern people. I want it *to tell* throughout the length and breadth of the land, so that whenever *Uncle Tom's Cabin* is mentioned, by an inevitable association men shall call up the Messenger's annihilation of its author. Such an article you can write, nor do I know any one who can do it but you — if you have not read it and will consent to review it, I will have it forwarded to you immediately — so that you can write the article in time for October.[9]

On September 11, 1852, (seventeen days later) Thompson again addressed Holmes, who had apparently agreed to write the review:

Pardon me for pointing out two or three absurdities in it for remark, which struck me. First, the design, avowed in the appendix to make war upon the

Fugitive Slave Act. This is treason against the Constitution. Second, the credit given the Ohio farmer for assisting the fugitives, in violation of his oath to support the Constitution. Third, the claim set up for the capacity of *the black race,* and their susceptibility of intellectual improvement, upon the faith of qualities manifested by George, Eliza & others, who are the children of *white men.* Fourth, the fact that Lagree the head devil of the book is a New England man by birth and education. Fifth, the palpable plagiarism of the story of Eva and Tom, *mutatis mutandis,* from Little Nell and her grandfather. Sixth, the direct falsehood involved in the statement put into the mouth of St. Clare, that there is no law in Louisiana against the murder of a slave by his master. These are only a few out of many which will no doubt suggest themselves to you at once. . . . [10]

Thompson's hopes were unrealized; Holmes's attack carried little weight, was little noticed, and did not arrive in time for either the October or November issues. Thompson himself then attempted to be "slashing" with only some success; but his failure was due largely to his lack of confidence in his own arguments. *Uncle Tom's Cabin* is a work of propaganda, more openly propagandistic than many of its kind. It was, therefore, easy to attack as a work of *belles lettres.* Thompson thus begins his editorial review by summarizing the plot, ridiculing in passing its social and legal implications as well as its ignorance of certain facts. He also points out the "feminist" proclivities, which "would place woman on a footing of political equality with men, . . . causing her to look beyond the office for which she was created." He charges Stowe with volunteering "officiously to intermeddle with things which concern her not — to libel and vilify a people from among whom have gone forth some of the noblest men that have adorned the race — to foment heartburnings and unappeasable hatred between brethren of a common country, the joint heirs of that country's glory." [11]

Next comes the logical rebuttal to three major points of Mrs. Stowe's abuse of the South. These are (1) "the cruel treatment of the slaves, (2) their lack of religious instruction, and (3) a wanton disregard of the sacred ties of consanguinity in selling members of the same family apart from each other." He then cites Southern laws against cruelty to slaves: "A code thus watchful of the negro's safety in life and limb, confines not its guardianship to inhibitory clauses, but proscribes extreme penalities in case of infraction."

Mrs. Stowe defended her novel in a long essay titled *The Key to Uncle Tom's Cabin,* which appeared in a remarkably short time considering the amount of research that evidently went into its preparation, much more than Thompson could possibly have done in the month or so that he had to write his article, which both in style and in thought reflects the great haste.[12] Mrs. Stowe concentrated her rebuttal on the disregard of the laws by slave owners and quoted from Southern journals and papers innumerable cases in which the law was circumvented. She turned Thompson's own case against him by pointed out in the case of "Souther vs. the Commonwealth," which Thompson had used as an example of Southern justice, very little justice was actually in evidence. She quoted the judge's statement of the crime:

The negro was tied to a tree and whipped with switches. Then Souther became fatigued with the labour of whipping, he called upon a negro man of his, and made him cob Sam with a shingle. He also made a negro woman of his help to cob him. And, after cobbing and whipping, he applied fire to the body of the slave. . . . He then caused him to be washed down with hot water, in which pods of red pepper had been steeped. The negro was also tied to a log and to the bedpost with ropes, which choked him, and he was kicked and stamped by Souther. This sort of punishment was continued and repeated until the negro died [the punishment having occupied about twelve hours] under its infliction.[13]

For this, Souther received a five-year sentence for second degree murder, because the jury thought "that it was [not] his design to kill the said slave, unless such design be properly inferable from the manner, means, and duration of the punishment." The jury was then moved to serious consideration of a new trial "upon the ground that the offense, if any, amounted only to manslaughter."[14] But justice prevailed!

Mrs. Stowe ignored Thompson's second point of argument, which had to do with the lack of religious training for Negroes; but his third point — separation of families — received extensive examination, copiously illustrated by examples and case histories.

Thompson's point was surely a weak one at best, since it was based on a Louisiana law which prohibited the sale of slave children under the age of ten years. Since "Eliza was eight or nine years old, when purchased, the story could not have taken place in Louisiana," Thompson declared triumphantly. A technicality at best, it is at worst a willful refusal to acknowledge the truth of Mrs. Stowe's parable of slavery. She in return, cited no less that one hundred advertisements for slaves of all ages: "Sixty-four Southern papers, taken 'at random' over a two-week period, contain advertisments of over four thousand Negroes for sale in 'choice' and selected lots.' " Is it possible, asked Mrs. Stowe, that such numbers will not involve "separation of families"? And what effect will such advertisements have on the mind of the young? She concluded that opinion in the South is "no more strenuous" in the slave's behalf than is the law "in any respect" effective in protecting him and that the system of slavery is generally destructive of the moral fiber of slave and slaveholder.

Finally, Mrs. Stowe replied to Thompson's assertion on the impossibility of the separation of Eliza from Cassy:

What is a law against the whole public sentiment of society? and will anybody venture to say that the public sentiment of Louisiana *practically* goes against separation of families?

But let us examine a case more minutely, remembering the bearing of it on two great foundation principles of slave jurisprudence: namely, that a slave cannot bring a suit in any case, except in a suit for personal freedom, and this in some States must be brought by a guardian; and that a slave cannot bear testimony in any case in which whites are implicated.

Suppose Butler wants to sell Cassy's child of nine years. There is a statute forbidding to sell under ten years; what is Cassy to do? She cannot bring suit. Will the State prosecute? Suppose it does; what then? Butler says the child is ten years old; if he pleases, he will say she is ten and a half, or eleven. What is Cassy to do? She cannot testify; besides, she is utterly in Butler's power. He may tell her that if she offers to stir in the affair, he will whip the child within an inch of its life; and she knows he can do it, and that there is no help for it; he may lock her up in a dungeon, sell her on to a distant plantation, or do any other despotic thing he chooses, and there is nobody to say — Nay.[14]

Round two to Mrs. Stowe!

In December of 1852, Holmes's article finally appeared. It is an interesting essay certainly, but as far as Thompson's hope of "blasting and searing the reputation of the vile wretch in petticoats" is concerned, it was utterly ineffective. The general thesis which dominates Holmes's paper, briefly noted in Thompson's original review, asserts that "heart rending separations are much less frequent under the institutions of slavery than in countries where poverty rules the working class with despotic sway. But admit the hardship to its full extent, and what does it prove? Evils are inseparable from all forms of society and this giant evil (if you will have it so) is more than counterbalanced by the advantages that Negroes enjoy."[15]

Holmes critized Mrs. Stowe for writing not fiction but a work of "proselytism," an idea even more literary than those used by Thompson, but one with which Thompson would not have agreed. Holmes declared that fiction "should have no significant bearing on life as it is actually lived" by insisting that it should be adorned in a "robe of ideal purity" properly suited to "the ever welcome companion of an idle hour." He also insisted that women should not step "beyond that hallowed precinct — the enchanted circle — which encompasses her with the halo of divinity." He ends his piece by urging, once more, the South to create a literature of its own: "The voice of a home-born literature, which would have been efficient in...defense is almost unheard, and if uttered, is scarcely noticed beyond the Mason and Dixon's line, because the Southern people have steadily refused to it that encouragement, both in the shape of material support and public favour, which is essential to its healthy development and assured existence, and which is imperatively required to give it respectability and influence abroad." Nor did Holmes's response to *The Key to Uncle Tom's Cabin,* two years later, add much to his original arguments.[16]

In his second essay, Holmes did not even try to dispute Mrs. Stowe's facts. He rather interpreted them to his own advantage. Holmes reaffirmed his original thesis — borrowed from Thompson's review — that slavery is like any other "social organization, civilized or savage.... The evils ascribed to the institution of slavery are incident in a still greater extent to all social organizations whatever, and...they are changed in form only while diminished in kind and degree by...its...prevalence.... Slavery only furnishes the occasion and determines the form of the brutality; it neither generates, nor would its abolition extricate it."[17] It is a sentiment worthy of what Veblen would call the quasi peaceable, semibarbarous man. No evidence was given in support, and his call to others to refute Mrs. Stowe, point by point, went unanswered.

Neither the arguments of Thompson nor of Holmes changed many opinions, but Thompson did gain some little notice from the North, for the *New York Day Book* did him the honor of stealing his little epigram on Mrs. Stowe.

> When Latin I studied, my Ainsworth in hand,
> I answered my teacher that *sto* meant to stand.

> But if asked, I should now give another reply,
> For *Stowe* means, beyond any cavil, to *lie*.[18]

Another point of interest in Thompson's first letter to Holmes has been omitted up to this point. It has to do with the financial problems of the magazine and its editor. In August 1852, Thompson wrote to Holmes, "Confidentially I must tell you I regard it as extremely doubtful whether the Messenger will survive December 1852." In 1850 he had written Augustan Taveau urging him to do what he could to increase the *Messenger's* subscription numbers, for "unless large accessions are made to the list before the 1st of January next, the Southern Literary Messenger, which has been in existence longer than any other periodical in America, will be stopped. For myself personally this is a matter of little consequence. I have sunk so far $5,000 in endeavoring to give the Southern people a magazine worthy of their fame and intellectual standing, and though I am willing to hazard no more, yet I shall not complain of them...."[19]

Now again in 1852, Thompson could not see how the *Messenger* could make it through another year. In other years of crisis, the *Messenger* had somehow continued and without alteration, but Thompson could not keep it going any longer. Almost miraculously, however, a solution was at hand in the *Messenger* office itself. The printers of the *Messenger,* MacFarlane and Fergusson, offered to buy Thompson's ownership and become the proprietors while Thompson remained as a salaried editor. It was at this time also, in an effort to bouy up the sales, that the yearly subscription rate was lowered from five to three dollars. Thompson had managed one more year to keep the *Messenger* issued regularly, and while his intention of keeping it nonpolitical had somewhat weakened, the *Messenger* was to continue as the least political journal in the South, if not in the nation.[20]

It was in this year, too, that Thompson made an early attempt to put together a book on Southern literature. Its tentative title was *Literature of the Southern States,* and its general design was that of an anthology of poetry with brief sketches of the authors and a general introduction. William Gilmore Simms seems to have been the prime mover in the venture. He urged Thompson to take on the job as compiler and proposed his name to a New York publishing house. Thompson outlined his plans to John Pendleton Kennedy in a letter, explaining his reasons for undertaking so great a task: "to do some little justice to Southern writers long treated with coldness and neglect by Northern critics, and to show that the Southern mind has been richly productive not only of those fruits upon which we have 'grown so great', but also of those rare and beautiful flowers which delight the eye and which shed fragrance around our homes.''[21] When notice of the proposed volume reached Griswold, he responded in his magazine, the *International*: "Mr. Thompson is a fine scholar, and has taste and a thorough acquaintance with the intellectual resources of the South, and his work will be interesting and valuable in many ways, though we suspect that it will fail of the accomplished editor's intent to show a general unfairness toward Southern writing by Northern critics.''[22] Thompson might have made a point by such a publication, particularly if he went back far enough to include Poe, and if he also included works by Southern writers which did appear in Northern magazines. If these two categories were omitted, however, his volume might have been rather shallow. It was a fact of economic simplicity; the *Messenger* could not afford to pay top prices so it had to settle for second and third-rate writers, except when, happily, Thompson discovered an unheralded writer of great talent. These he could not keep once their reputations had been established. Such was universally the case with journals of the South. Be this as it may, it can never be known what Thompson might have accomplished, for he never published the book. Why has not been revealed.

Certainly the contents of the *Messenger* during these years might have discouraged him, for with little money to pay he had to resort to filling the pages with quotations, with tales and articles from other magazines, and articles on William Gilmore Simms, Frances Lieber of South Carolina, and on William and Mary College taken from Evert and George Duyckinck's *Cyclopedia of American Literature*. He reprinted whole sketches and culled quotations from newspapers, weeklies, novels, and histories. Since even buying American magazines was more than he could afford, he often begged his friends in the North to send him bundles of used magazines from Europe — these he could plead were not available in the South. He wrote reviews using long excerpts; numerous essays from his own pen also appeared anonymously, as did his poetry. Finally he resorted to printing orations and speeches — some of his own, others from Joseph G. Baldwin, Henry A. Wise, expresident John Tyler, James Barron Hope, John Pendleton

Kennedy, and St. George Tucker, and others who were willing to have their speeches appear in print.

Thompson was always busy and the added burden of writing his own material and hunting out inexpensive copy added greatly to his obligations. Still, he occasionally had time to spare for the events around him, as an informal letter to Cooke indicates:

Office dull, hot Sunday afternoon — 'all alone by myself' — cigar about two-thirds gone — why should I not write to acknowledge your last letter? I will — For a week past Richmond has been exceedingly stupid — the weather, five days out of seven, rainy, and none but gloomy events to break in upon the monotony of our existence. Thursday the funeral of the unhappy victims of the Reindeed casualty took place.... The next day — Friday — Jane Williams was hung in accord with her sentence. The usual number of devil's children assembled in Horse-Heaven Hollow and Gallows Glen to enjoy her dying agonies and get that improvement of the moral sense which Hugh Pleasants says, in a recent number of the Dispatch, never fails to attend the witnessing of such exhibitions. Butchertown turned out its negroes and Cary Street its strumpets, and between them the poor wretch Jane was bravely attended upon her last ride on earth.[23]

Jane Williams was a slave who had murdered with axes and knives all of the members of her master's family except the master himself. She was tried immediately and sentenced to death; the sentence was carried out about two months after the murder. Thompson's attitude toward the hanging of Jane Williams is rather at varience with the attitude taken in his support of slavery as expressed, for example, in his essays on Lowell and Mrs. Stowe. There is even a touch of the macabre irony of Jonathan Swift, at the end of the letter.

If Thompson did not have enough to worry about with the "gloomy events" and the difficulty with the *Messenger,* B. B. Minor suggests that he might also have been in love. In a note which is not dated but comes on the same page with the catalogue of happenings in 1852, Minor says, apropo of nothing, "Mr. Thompson, however, was willing to marry. The accomplished lady whose hand he tried to win married quite late a widower with several children. She is now [1905] an elite widow, with nothing but step-children, and is very highly esteemed."[24] This unnamed lady may have been Miss Lucy Haxall, whom Thompson had courted in the 1840s. He was still among the group of suitors who met at her father's house during the Civil War. Miss Haxall did marry late and had at least one stepchild. There is another possibility mentioned by Augustin Taveau, in a letter of February 29, 1852:

I had the pleasure of being in company, a few evenings since, with one of your Virginia belles, Miss Rutherford [*sic.*]: of whom I am free to confess that if she is a fair specimen of your Ladies generally, Virginia must be a very dangerous place for most Gentlemen of Carolina! She spoke very kindly of you to me, and betrayed one or two of your "affairs de coeur," which, be assured, I shall keep with rigid sanctity.[25]

On March 3, just four days later, Thompson answered,

I am sure the gentle loveliness of my fair friend Miss Emily Rutherfoord will create very sincere admiration among the cultivated young gentlemen of Charleston. Virginia certainly could not have anywhere a more charming representative, and I count the privilege of her acquaintance among the chief blessings of my Richmond nativity and residence. If she has informed you of any "little weaknesses" of mine, I am very glad to say that I cannot return the compliment, for she has no weaknesses of any sort.[26]

But if this was the lady referred to by Minor, there is no further evidence to support the idea. Thompson did not marry, though he seems, over the years, to have paid not too earnest courtship to several belles.

The year 1853 was not an easy one for Thompson, for his work mounted; he was no longer his own boss, and his health was failing. It was, however, a good year in one respect, for it was then that he met the English novelist, William Makepeace Thackeray who was touring the country on his first American visit, his lectures hailed as a treat *par excellence*. Thompson, who was always in the thick of Richmond's cultural and entertainment events, had almost singlehandedly brought Jenny Lind to Richmond some years earlier. Now he wrote to Thackeray offering the Richmond Athenaeum and his own services as advance man. Thackeray accepted the offer and requested the evening of the "28th and the three next open ensuing nights." He remained in Richmond a week, delighting in Thompson's company and spending much of his time in the *Messenger* office, where he discussed literature generally and his own in particular. He told Thompson that he was willing "to be judged as a writer by *Henry Esmond*"; and it was here during a discussion of Goethe's novel — which was the year's *cause celebrete* — that he wrote for Thompson his comic poem on "The Sorrows of Werther."[27]

The year before his visit, Thackeray had composed his lecture series on "The Eighteenth-Century Humorists": these he delivered in the United States in 1852-1853. Mrs. Mary N. Stanard wrote of the author's Virginia visit:

For at least part of the time his hostess was Mrs. Robert C. Stanard (whose husband had been Poe's schoolmate and chum) in the house which is now the Westmoreland Club. He stayed a week this time during which he delivered to audiences which packed the Athenaeum on Marshall Street, near Eleventh, three lectures on literary subjects: "Swift"; "Congrave and Addison," and "Steele and the Times of Queen Anne." On March 3rd, he wrote from Richmond to Mrs. Baxter, of New York, of being "Delighted with the comfortable, friendly, cheery little town — the picturesque" he had seen in America. He added, "I am having a good time — pleasant people, good audiences, quiet, handsome, cheap, comfortable hotel" — evidently the "Exchange.". . . On March 12th he wrote from Charleston: "From this I shall go to Richmond most probably, and say my say out there; if their enthusiasm lasts four weeks I am sure of a great welcome at that pretty little cheery place — such as is better than dollars." He stayed on another week and lectured on "Prior, Gay, and Pope"; "Hogarth, Smollet, and Fielding," and "Stern and Goldsmith."[28]

Between Thackeray and Thompson, the liking was immediate, mutual and strong. They were entertained together by Mrs. Stanard, whose husband and son were close friends of Thompson, and Thompson gave a stag party for the distinguished visitor at his father's house. Thackeray, who was a collector of rocking chairs, made a gift of one to Thompson, noting in the presentation, "I saw your Rocker was in délabre condition and bought a two-penny one which I beg you to sit in sometimes and smoke a cigar and think (as I shall of your kindness)."[29] They met again in England in 1854 and again when Thackeray returned to the United States in 1856. Thompson later attributed Thackeray's sympathy with the South during the Civil War to the friendships which he held with so many Southerners; Thackeray's son-in-law, Sir Leslie Stephens, agreed with Thompson's conclusion.

Later that year Thompson traveled north in the company of Joseph G. Baldwin, author of *Flush Times of Alabama and*

Mississippi and other works of comic genius, to attend the opening
of the Crystal Palace, go to the opera, and see the sights. Baldwin
had met Thompson through his articles written for the *Messenger,*
and Thompson took pleasure in showing his young friend around.
Here they met President Pierce, for whose election John M. Daniel
had worked in Richmond. The trip was typical of the many which
Thompson took to entertain his friends and fellow writers. In a
long list of friends who traveled with Thompson since he became
editor, some of the more prominent were N. P. Willis, John
Pendleton Kennedy, Philip Pendleton Cook and John Esten
Cooke, and Paul Hamilton Hayne. But after that trip to New York
the jaunts became fewer, and his absences from Richmond more
often for reasons of failing health rather than the pursuit of
pleasure.[30]

Thompson had suffered from tuberculosis for a number of
years, and from 1852 on the attacks had become more debilitating.
His family and friends had urged him to take a long holiday, but
the press of business had been too urgent. He was eager to make his
mark and wished to publish something in book form. In the spring
of that year he had set about the enormous task of preparing the
anthology of Southern literature of "not less in bulk than 500
Messenger pages," and had failed. Perhaps it was due to his poor
health, or perhaps the failure and its resulting distress aggravated
his condition. In any case he struggled through 1853 with declining
health.

The year 1854 opened with hope of a new beginning. The
Editor's Table in the January issue was full of thanks and
congratulations to the subscribers, whose numbers had shown a
recent and encouraging increase. With the assurance that the
Messenger would survive another year, Thompson's health
improved — but then it also seems cool weather always helped.
However, he experienced a relapse, and in the spring of 1854 his
father, whose financial affairs were much improved, offered to
send his son to Europe for a long rest. Thompson had long desired
to see Europe and visit the places of literary and historical fame. So
on the twenty-sixth of April, Thompson was issued a passport on
which he was described as "thirty years of age, five feet six and one
quarter inches in height, with low forehead, gray eyes, straight
nose, square chin, brown hair, fair complexion and oval face."[31]
His ship sailed on the thirteenth of May. In a long letter to his
friend John Esten Cooke, who had again taken on the job of

temporary editor of the *Messenger,* Thompson would describe his trip:

Five days on the water establishes relations of pleasant familiarity among the passengers. Congenial circles are formed, in accordance with the taste of the parties. A knot of stout old gentlemen, members of the New York and Boston clubs, play incessant whist at a guinea a corner, and snub an occasional new hand for an unfortunate finesse. Another circle smokes, sings, and in smooth water, plays shuffleboard under the auspices of Mr. Chips, the carpenter. It is a braw party, this. Gallant Alabama Colonel, distinguished for exploits in the Mexican War, generous and gay. — Kind John Bull, going home on a visit from his American fireside, devoted to all the Muses, and an artist in the way of punches. Philadelphia importers, en route for the manufacturing districts of Europe, and worthy representatives of the City of Brotherly Love. Young M.D.'s going to Paris — Such were some of the component parts of the loveliest coterie of our local load.[32]

Thirteen days on the Atlantic and the ship landed at Liverpool, and Thompson, ever mindful of his editorial demands, had met at least one man of letters on board about whom he could write in the *Messenger.* This was Colonel James W. Wall, author of *Foreign Etchings or Outline Sketches of Pleasant Places in the World.* Thompson hardly needed any more incentive to write about his travels, but if he had, Colonel Wall just may have provided it.

From Liverpool he took the train south "through the fairest of meadows, by Tamworth, with its momentary glimpse of Drayton Manor — the residence of Sir Robert Peel, and through Rugby, suggestive of Dr. Arnold, until getting nearer the great metropolis, it passed directly under Harrow on the Hill, memorable as the scene of Byron's school days." London, which impressed the poet with its magnificence, its history and its ghosts, made him feel the fullness of Dr. Johnson's remark: "Sir, when a man is tired of London he is tired of life; for there is in London all that life can afford."

Thompson was elated to be in London; he walked the streets viewing the old with young eyes and the new as well. On his first full day in London he strolled over to the new Houses of Parliaments, where the discussion by the Lords of a railway bill did not interest him as much as the Lords themselves. On Derby Day he was one of the "miscellaneous two hundred thousand who went to Epsom Downs to enjoy that brave spectacle," and where his own fine clothes would seem inconspicuous in the affluence of European society. He travelled with friends in an "old-fashioned English stage-coach, such as the Elder Weller was proud to drive, with four splendid grays, a 'nobby turn out' as one of our jockeys said," over the seventeen miles of beautiful macadamized highway. There were many delays on the crowded road, and on one occasion the group uncorked a bottle of claret. On another, Thompson found his coach beside one which contained a party led by his famous acquaintance of the previous year, William M. Thackeray. Acquaintances were renewed, and Thompson was much impressed by the races, run every hour, with a lunch — "a feast to set before Victoria" — in between. From the fullness of the provisions he entertained "two good-looking boys of the Blue Coat School, who had walked all the way from London to make me remember with gratitude the gentle Elia who once wore their quaint uniform."

Back in London he visited Westminster and of it wrote to Cooke:

It was not until I had been a week in London, and had become quite familiar with the venerable towers of Westminster that I entered the Abbey.... The interior is certainly imposing, but the hand of time which ordinarily heightens the effect, by mellowing the tone of architectural masterpieces, had so defaced the details of the Abbey with mould, as to render them very unsightly. The fine windows alone, fully met my expectations.[33]

As he roamed through the great buildings and read the inscriptions of the great men commemorated there, he was finally filled with awe and reverence. Later he joined in an excursion to Hampton Court to see the old palace and returned by Richmond and its deer park, then on to dinner at the "Star and Garter," which was delightful for its company and food. Years later, writing for the *Messenger,* Thompson would recall his memories of the delightful twilight looking down from the terrace on the silver Thames bordered by emerald meadows.

Thackeray had just returned from Italy when Thompson renewed his acquaintance; in the three weeks before Thackeray departed for Bologne to finish *The Newcomes,* he entertained Thompson at Onslow Place, where the young editor met numerous literary folk. Most importantly, he met Thackeray's elder daughter, Anne. It was the beginning of another lifelong friendship, the depths of which no record has yet revealed.

Among the men Thompson came to know at this time, probably none inspired more immediate respect than Samuel Rogers. With him Thompson was honored to have a breakfast which he described in some detail:

There is perhaps no breakfast table in the two continents that has had seated around it, at various times, so much of intellectual greatness — indeed, a breakfast with the poet Rogers has been for years the most desirable of delights to the man of letters. We once enjoyed this privilege, and though age had somewhat dimmed the perceptions of the poet and the lameness, the result of a serious accident late in life rendered it necessary for him to be wheeled to the table in his chair, we shall not soon forget the richness of that conversation which ranged through the reminiscences of more than half a century of intimate communion with the most re-markable men of the modern world. The man who had seen and known Samuel Johnson and was the contemporary of George Washington, who had heard Sheridan in the highest flights of his oratory and in the most brilliant flashes of his wit, who had watched the career of Napoleon from the first to the last, and who was the familiar friend of Scott, Byron, and Wordsworth, could not fail, while he retained his faculties, to be more entertaining in his Table Talk than any score of biographies.[34]

Between visits with famous personalities, Thompson attended the Annual Exhibition of the Royal Academy, strolled through Hyde and Kensington Parks, and travelled to the great houses in and around London. Among the friends with whom he shared his love of England were Henry Winter Davis and Robert E. Randall, two Americans who joined him for most of the remainder of his European junket.

The three young Americans went on to Paris, where they spent five weeks "visiting the more interesting and memorable sights and scenes of the wonderful metropolis," which was at this time being developed even more under the Emperor. Perhaps more interesting even than the Place de la Concorde, Bois de Boulogne, and Versailles was the Frenchman's love of food. Lengthy descriptions of incidents in French cafes and of "the Frenchman's art of eat-ing" are included in Thompson's letters of this period. He was also inspired to write two poems, "In Forma Pauperis" and "La Morgue." And it was here that he met the young Bulwer, the first Earl of Lytton, and read the proof sheets of *Clytemnestra* and its companion poems, first published in 1855, at which time Thompson reviewed the book in the *Messenger.* He was favorably impressed with the poet — then known as Owen Meredith — and pre-dicted that he would someday produce something of great worth.[35]

Early in July the trio went on to Brussels. Here Thompson was so entranced by the points made famous in Charlotte Bronte's *Villetta* and Thackeray's *Vanity Fair* that he hardly noticed the charm of the little city: "Instead of looking around me for the actual sights mentioned in the guidebooks, I came very near calling for a valet de place to show me the lodgings where Jos Sedley cut off his mustaches and the chambers hallowed by the grief of Amelia Osbornc aftcr Watcrloo." Of course, the group visited the battle-field and the nearby Cathedral of St. Gugule, where, on the Sunday Thompson and his friends were there, the ceremonies com-memorating the sacrilege of the Jews against the consecrated wafers were performed. The pagentry was awe inspiring.

From Brussels, they traveled through Mechlin, famous for its lace, to Antwerp:

A quaint old city it certainly is, with its absurd gables, its odd porches, its crooked streets leading into all manner of labyrinthine perplexities, its remarkable Bourse, where in the balmy days of Flemish prosperity, the solid men of Antwerp were accustomed to regulate the trade of Europe, and as the stranger walks through its wide places, and under the shadow of its antiquated warehouses, all his reading of it, in history and fiction, comes back to him, and it seems to him that it would not be at all extra-ordinary if the characters of long ago, real and imaginary, the old burgo-masters of the painters and Quentin Durward, should suddenly pop around the nearest corner and take off their sombreros in passing.[36]

They visited the rooms where Rubens painted some of his best works, the museums, the cathedral, the Church of St. Jacques, and took rambles around the city.

After three days they forced themselves to leave "the sixteenth century we knew in Antwerp." They were bound for Rotterdam and then the Hague: "By an unlucky chance, it turned out that other great people besides ourselves were enroute for the Hague that day — the young king of Portugal and his suite — and had made choice of the Hotel Bellevue for lodging." They did find lesser accommodations for their brief stay and went on to Delft and Leyden, to Amsterdam, which Thompson found "positively great fun" because of its canals, curious shops, windows draped with embroidered curtains, "amphibious looking babies who tottered on the very brink of the water — everything was singular, extra-ordinary, mirth-provoking." After Arnheim, by boat to Düsseldorf, Thompson took a train to Cologne, Weisbaden,

Goethe's Frankfort, Baden-Baden, and then Berlin. He was repeatedly inspired to recollections of the literary associations in these spots, of Thackeray's Mr. Titmarsh and Lord Byron, who had followed much the same European journey of education. In Berlin the usually reliable Davis discovered he had lost the claim tickets, but a forgiving group of inspectors allowed the trio to retrieve their trunks. The situation became one more of the amusing anecdotes which Thompson had to write about in his diary and letters.

From Berlin the three Americans traveled through Dresden, Vienna, Nussdorf, Munich, Ausburg, Lindan, Zurich to Geneva, where, after learning that the cholera epidemic in Italy had lessened, Thompson left his cotravellers and went south to Florence. There he joined the large company of American artists and their families. He was readily accepted into the artistic community and spent many pleasant days in the studios of Powers, Read, and Hart and talked with poets and scholars, of whom he wrote:

If the conversation of authors in private might be mentioned with as much freedom as the works of artists, I would refer here to the literary circle of Florence, and tell of a delightful evening with Lever, the author of Charles O'Malley and of a talk with Mrs. Browning who was anxious to hear all I could tell her of Poe.[37]

It may have been this conversation with Mrs. Browning that moved Thompson to write, some six years later, his lecture on Poe, for the Brownings were quite eager to see Poe's memory vindicated and said so to Thompson.[38]

A fortnight was then spent in Rome, where Thompson concentrated his attention on St. Peter's, the Coliseum, the Capagna and the Apollo. Once again he quickly made friends among the American colony and visited the studios of Gibson, Crawford, and C. G. Thompson, the Boston artist. Two weeks was too short a time in Rome, but Thompson had yet to see Naples before starting his homeward journey. Then the trip was over.

In a few weeks after I had lain extended on the side of the volcano drinking in the inspiration of the lovely locality, I was at home again, looking back upon Europe, with its pomps and pageants, its cathedrals and alps, its sweet paintings and sunny landscapes, as a dream.[39]

During the next two years, Thompson revised the many letters he had sent back to Cooke and the *Messenger,* added to them some unpublished material from his diary, and sent the manuscript to New York for publication. The printed book was sent to the bindery of Derby and Jackson, where, a day before it was due to be released, a fire — the famous New York conflagration of 1856 — wiped out the bindery and burned every copy of the book, including proof sheets. Since the publishing company was already in financial straits, it made no effort to reprint the book, which was titled *Across the Atlantic.* A remarkable piece of luck ensued, however. Several days after the fire, a printer discovered in a desk drawer an unbound copy; he had it bound in "exquisite style," and sent it to the author as a small compensation for his loss. Thompson placed the book in a position of honor on his shelves and referred to it as "a literary curiosity — being the only volume he had ever seen of which there was but a single copy in existence." And in the Editor's Table for the *Messenger* he consoled himself.

Whatever personal disappointment the editor may have experienced on this account, was more than compensated by the prompt and voluntary expression of sympathy which came to him from friends. He found also a consolation in reflecting, that perhaps the conflagration had saved him a scorching from the critics, that the work had probably anticipated its inevitable doom, and that at least the edition had gone off rapidly and brilliantly.[40]

Thompson's health seemed completely restored, the tuberculosis arrested. He plunged himself back into the social, business, and cultural affairs of Richmond. In February he presented an address at the Atheneaum on "Paris in Its External Aspects." Five days later he was addressing the Central Mount Vernon Association and its friends and urging that George Washington's home be purchased for preservation to be made a memorial of the country's first president. Among his numerous other offices and duties in Richmond, Thompson also served as corresponding secretary of the association. Later he appeared with James Barron Hope and B. Johnson Barber at a fair sponsored by the Mechanic's Institute of Richmond, for which he had purchased a copy of Guido's "Beatrice Cenci," the original of which hangs in the Barberini Palace in Rome. This painting was one of the major attractions in the October meeting in 1855. On November 1, he was reported by the Richmond *Dispatch* to have spoken on "Conservative

Influence of the Mechanic Arts upon Society," an address "happily selected for the occasion, and...discussed with decided ability." Thompson seems almost always to have been a successful lecturer; he had an immense fund of information and a keen ability to adapt his material to his needs. Most importantly, he understood his audiences and seldom, if ever, spoke above their heads. He was witty and personable and attractive, but did not awe his listeners nor digress from their interests into arcane subjects. Finally, he avoided controversial subjects for the most part. He did not spur his audience to action or rebellion; he made them at ease, and he entertained them.

His poetry was also a popular form of oral presentation. Thompson was, for example, invited to recite his poem "Patriotism" before the national convention of the Delta Kappa Epsilon fraternity, which met in Richmond on January 3, 1856.[41] Later, in February, he delivered the poem again at the Athenaeum. It is rather jinglely, timely, humorous, and patriotic, striking just the right note for such occasions — as one should expect from occasional poetry. On the third of July, again by invitation, he read his poem "Virginia" before the Phi Beta Kappa Society of William and Mary College at Williamsburg. In three thousand lines of open couplets he praised Virginia, paid tribute to his late friend Philip Cooke, and lamented the death of Edgar Allan Poe. The concluding paragraph is typical.

> What tho' they say Virginia lags behind
> Her rival sisters in the March of the Mind?
> What tho' so frequently 'tis ours to hear
> The pointless jest, the miserable sneer,
> From men, whose freedom 'twas her joy to save,
> Or States, whose every inch of soil she gave?
> If some sweet lethargy has sealed her lips
> And quenched her vision in a brief eclipse;
> And on the pedestal of former fame —
> Whose proud inscription is her simple name —
> She long has stood in statuesque repose,
> Pure as if hewn from everlasting snows,
> 'Tis as Hermione, the peerless Queen,
> The glorious image, stood in Shakespeare's scene;
> Soon shall the form descend, no more be stone,
> With flowering drapery and flashing zone,
> Walk forth in majesty, Minerva-like,
> And all who look on her with marvel strike![42]

By order of the Phi Beta Kappa, the poem was published by Thompson's own printers as a pamphlet.

Again, on February 3, 1857, Thompson appeared as a speaker for the benefit of the poor of the city who had suffered during an unusually severe winter; on this occasion his talk at the Athenaeum was on "European Journalism." He had already given at least one lecture in the series which had brought his old friend William Gilmore Simms to Richmond on February 28.

The outstanding occasion on which Thompson spoke, during these years of the late 1850s, was the day of celebration of Washington's birthday in 1858. This was the day on which Crawford's statue of Washington was unveiled to the public.[43] The incomplete statue had arrived on the Walborg on November 15, 1857, from Amsterdam, and the city had waited in anxious anticipation for it to be unloaded. Curiously, it was not until winter had arrived that the box containing the statue was raised to the deck. The word was immediately spread, and great crowds of people rushed to the dock to catch a glimpse of the statue. Eventually the statue was placed on a wagon and hauled toward the Capitol grounds, but the twelve horses pulling it were stopped by the throng of people at Seventeenth Street. The horses were unhitched amid great shouts of joy, and the citizens pulled the wagon on to the Capitol, cheering and laughing. Two local companies of young guards fired salutes; Governor Wise and the Richmond mayor made impromptu speeches. The statue then remained enshrouded until February, when Thompson and James Barron Hope read original odes. Simms read Thompson's ode in the *Messenger* and wrote, congratulating him "on the real beauty of your inauguration Poem. It is exceedingly happy."[44]

The *Messenger* continued to consume most of Thompson's time and energy, and he frequently found it necessary to escape the work, the pressure, and the heat of Richmond. For even a healthy man, Thompson maintained a relentless pace of writing, speaking, editing, and socializing, which he felt obligated to keep up even though he usually enjoyed all kinds of get-togethers. In the late summer of 1858 he apologized for the lateness of the September number, writing in the Editor's Table of his visit to Berkeley Springs:

We shall not readily forget the August idleness of 1858. There is something very enjoyable in this sort of existence, filled up with nothings, that one passes at a watering-place which is neither too crowded for comfort, nor too "fast" for the quiet needed by the city fugitive seeking relaxation.[45]

Or was it his consumption returning? Another trip occurred in 1859, which was more active, when he was a guest of the Baltimore and Ohio Railway along with a distinguished company which included the Boston jurist Judge George W. Warren, Commander Matthew Fontaine Maury, N. P. Willis, Bayard Taylor, and John Pendleton Kennedy. Their charter train stopped along the way for sightseeing and fishing. On another excursion Thompson joined a group of sixteen ladies and gentlemen, including Edward E. Everrett, on a trip to Jamestown. On the way the group was entertained at the Brandon plantation, about which Thompson would later write one of his more popular poems.

Financial worries had not been forgotten, however. The *Messenger* was still making little profit, if any, for its owners — now MacFarlane and Fergusson. In 1856 they had changed the format of the magazine, reducing the always cumbrous size of the pages, but increasing the number of them so that more material was presented in a more convenient form, thus making more work for the editor. The resulting thickness of the issues made it difficult to bind twelve issues in a volume, as many libraries and private subscribers did. Consequently, a new series was begun with the January volume of 1856. That first volume ended with June, and thereafter the *Messenger* was printed as two volumes per year (1856 included volumes XXII and XXIII). But nothing seemed to keep the subscription numbers high enough to guarantee a profit, not even lowering the yearly rate from five to three dollars, which had been done in 1853.

In the spring of 1859, Thompson began to look for employment that would require less strenuous effort and pay better; it also seems that he did not consider his employment under MacFarlane and Fergusson satisfactory. In June of 1860 he wrote Dr. George W. Bagby, "Strictly entre nous, I was never fairly treated by M & F [MacFarlane and Fergusson]. They neglected the magazine utterly — didn't seem to care a d—n whether it succeeded or not — never paid a cent for my labours — and did not even so much as come to say good-bye! to me, before I left home."[46] Thompson had written to John P. Kennedy on the twenty-first of March about the position of librarian at the Peabody Institute in Baltimore. Apparently Kennedy had originated the correspondence about the job, but

Thompson was most eager in his pursuit of the position. Many letters of recommendation were written on Thompson's behalf at this time by men of distinguished reputation; among these were letters from the faculties of the University of Virginia, William and Mary and the Virginia Military Institute, and from as far away as Boston, where Edward Everett and G. Washington Warren wrote. But the debate in the selection committee dragged on through the first half of 1860.

Before the choice was made in Baltimore, Thompson received an offer from James Gardner, proprietor of the *Southern Field and Fireside* of Augusta, Georgia, asking him to accept the position of editor of that journal "with a salary of Two Thousand Dollars a year...."[47] The current editor of the Georgia magazine was W. W. Mann, whom Thompson had hired as a correspondent for the *Messenger* in 1847, but Thompson had been in correspondence with the proprietor in 1859, for he had written recommending Dr. Bagby for the editorship. What seems then to have happened was that W. W. Mann asked Thompson to recommend someone to Gardner, and Thompson named Bagby, who had been writing for the *Messenger* recently. For some reason the proprietor delayed making any decision on the editorship until the next year, when he heard that Thompson himself was looking for a change of positions. Gardner then asked Thompson to make an immediate decision and offered him a salary well neigh unheard of in magazine circles. But Thompson did not want to live so far from home, particularly since warm weather seems to have irritated his consumptive lungs. He received Gardner's letter on the twenty-second of March 1860, almost exactly a year after he had first written to Kennedy about the Peabody Institute position. He immediately sent off a note assuring Kennedy that he much preferred the Baltimore librarianship, but that he was expected to answer Gardner by the twenty-fourth. Twelve hours after Thompson had written to accept the Georgia offer, Kennedy's answer arrived, delayed in transit. In any case, it only said that a decision had not been reached. In his letter to Kennedy, Thompson explained his situation.

I accepted the overture under a strong compulsion of debt and res angusta — not Augusta. My life has not been a fortunate one. My father — the most indulgent of fathers, who at one time was independent, worth his hundred thousand dollars, had been impoverished. The *Messenger,* which

I took in better days, has proved a dead loss to me — ever so much money actually sunk and twelve years of early manhood spent unprofitably in maintaining it. At 36 I must commence life anew.[48]

On March 25, however, he was still hoping for the Baltimore job and wrote Kennedy,

I dare say I could get off from my Georgia engagement before any announcement is made of my accession to the Editorial chair of the journal in question. What think you of this? Of course, I desire to act in good faith, and if, in your opinion, my acceptance of the Georgia offer makes necessary the withdrawal of my application to your Board, then you will consider this letter as a formal request to withhold the papers already filed and consider me 'out of the ring'. If there should seem to you no impropriety in allowing the credentials to remain until the appointment is made (supposing this will be done speedily) with the knowledge that I should greatly prefer to come to Baltimore than to go to Augusta, why things had better remain as they are.[49]

Kennedy was chairman of the committee, and Thompson was his choice, but he would not have tried to persuade the Board to vote his way. When the vote was finally taken, Dr. John G. Morris, a member of the committee, was elected. Of the eight candidates, Dr. Morris received ten votes and Thompson four.[50]

Thompson thus resigned from the *Messenger* and prepared to move to Augusta, but first his successor was to be found. In January of 1859, the *Messenger* had published an essay, "It is Omnipotent," by the former Lynchburg, Virginia, newspaper editor, Dr. George W. Bagby. In the May number, he published again — this time under the famous pseudonym, Mozis Addums; then as G. Buggini Wufficks he wrote sketches for the June, July, and November numbers; a satirical essay titled "The Polite Art of Noveling: A Didactic Fiction" ended the series. In the next year he seemed willing to put his theories of fiction to the test and published his only novel, *Blue-Eyes and Battlewick: A Winter's Tale,* a half-humorous but creaking allegory that ran in serial form from January to May, 1860. He was Thompson's last literary find for the *Messenger.* It was to Dr. Bagby that the editorship was now offered, at Thompson's suggestion. It was not, for Dr. Bagby, a moment of unmitigated joy. On accepting the offer, he wrote to Miss Ellen Turner:

I am to take charge of the *Messenger* when Thompson leaves. This compels me to give up the Library business, except so far as the Historical Society is concerned, and gives me more writings to do, when I have already enough in all conscience. The pay is trifling — only $300 a year, and the books sent to be reviewed, say 150 volumes a year at the outside, and most of them of no intrinsic value. My fear — nay my assurance is that I shall have the honor of assisting at the death of the *Messenger* as I did with the *Express* and *Courier* in Lynchberg. But there is no help for it.[51]

It was now Bagby's duty to bid a public farewell to the former editor, who had been his personal friend since Thompson first met him in Lynchburg some years before. So in his first essay as editor he wrote of his predecessor:

The great service rendered to the *Messenger* by Mr. Thompson, during the long period of his connection with it, can be understood only by those who know something of the manifold difficulties of the position he assumed. When he took charge of it he was but a boy.... What guarantee was there that the magazine, then, as now, one of the first in the Union, would be conducted properly? Let the pages of the *Messenger* during the past thirteen years be the answer. It is but the simple statement of fact to say that the arduous task of conducting a leading magazine has been accomplished by Mr. Thompson with signal success. The unknown aspirant for literary honours in 1847, leaves the *Messenger* in 1860, a man distinguished in every part of the Confederacy, in the North scarcely less than in the South, as a poet, a scholar, a lecturer, and editor. It is in this last capacity — as editor — that he has to our thinking discovered the highest intellectual and personal qualities.[52]

Thompson's career of thirteen years, the longest for any editor of the *Messenger,* was at an end. After numerous farewell parties and expressions of respect from his fellow townsmen, Thompson left Richmond and went north to Baltimore for a day, then on to New York for the Irving celebration on April 3. On his return to Richmond he found waiting for him an offer of a speaking tour by the Harrison Literary Institute, but he felt compelled to go on to Augusta. Once there he wrote back to Kennedy:

I did not have a chance to write you from Richmond before my departure because of the numberless distractions incident to breaking up and getting ready for flight. Besides the ordinary leave takings and P.P.C.'s of the social circle, I was honoured with a complimentary Dinner by my friends.[53]

Arranged by twenty-nine of Thompson's friends, led by William H. MacFarlane, of the old Whig Party days, this dinner was especially grand. Among the invited guests were J. E. Cooke, Dr. H. G. Latham of Lynchburg, and Dr. Bagby. Thompson, who loved all such gatherings, must have been moved by this one, by the toasts and speeches of appreciation, by a song written for the occasion and sung by his old friend Dr. C. Bell Gibson. Nevertheless, the next day he would have to leave Richmond, and that thought may have made all the rest seem empty. Dr. Bagby, writing the next month in the *Messenger,* touched on one of Thompson's most persistent qualities, his love of home and country:

We are glad that Virginia's loss is Georgia's gain, but we are unwilling to believe that these cordial Southerners can win his heart from his native State. Virginian he is, Virginian he must remain. Be his home where it may, let his taste and talents find fitting rewards in what State they may, he shall not forget the beautiful city that gave him birth and the notable Commonwealth, whom he has already honoured and whom he will honour yet more in years to come.[54]

These were prophetic words.

CHAPTER 4

Thompson's Criticism and Poetry

THOMPSON'S achievement as a writer and critic during his days with the *Southern Literary Messenger* was not inconsiderable. As critic and editor — and the two jobs are inseparable here — Thompson possessed several necessary attributes, none of them brilliant but all competent and useful. He had endurance, despite his struggle with consumption. He kept the *Messenger* going longer than any other Southern magazine at that time — longer than any in the united States of its type except the *Knickerbocker,* which, founded in 1833, was less than a year older. Doubtless the fact that he had the financial backing of his father at crucial times during the early years of his editorship was important. Yet Thompson was a resourceful man, and for several years of his tenure as editor, each year of existence was a matter of his own remarkable ability to generate support from what to others seemed a hopelessly indifferent public. He endured, and he was tactful. Dr. Bagby wrote of him in 1860:

We venture the assertion that few men ever had control for so long a time of a periodical, who have given less offense and more general satisfaction than Mr. Thompson. If his kindness has been appreciated by contributors, and especially by those just beginning the up-hill way of literary life, his discriminations, his judgment, and above all his pure taste, have excited the warm approbation of cultivated and refined readers.[1]

That testimony tells much about Thompson's reasons for success and failure. Had his taste been less refined, he might have done better, but this was a matter of his own judgment. Bagby, who followed, did not do much better at a time when things were very propitious for Southern publications. And Bagby did not reflect that refined taste. For example, Thompson wrote to him in 1858 objecting to a bedroom scene in the seventh letter of Addum Mozis, finding it too suggestive, ending with "Perhaps I am a prude."[2] Three days later, he wrote again, "I suggested it to you first because of my sensitivity on the point of immodesty (in print, mind you, where my sister is going to read it, and not as a matter of fun for myself who am past injury by Pagauet, Louvet, Paul de Kock, Mrs. Dudevant or any of them — not forgetting Miss Lizzie Petit herself) d--n the parenthesis and 2nd there are certain smart critics...."[3] Thompson's policy as editor and critic had been relatively successful. Only Poe had been more effective at bringing the *Southern Literary Messenger* to so many people. Poe had the genius of his own mind as an attraction, but then much of his popularity was due to his "slashing" of Northern writers — no matter that he slashed the writers of the South; the South was used to that. But it was a unique and very satisfying experience to read a Southern journal which with real literary merit and upon genuine literary grounds so lambasted the best and most pretentious of the Northern writers.

Thompson was not temperamentally suited to that kind of criticism, as his two attempts at the vitriolic style testify. One of these was the review of *Uncle Tom's Cabin,* already discussed. The other was occasioned by a very weak poem, "The Fairy of the Stream,"[4] written by a pretentious young Richmond lawyer named Farmer. For once in his published work, Thompson expressed his outrage at the presumption of an incompetent writer. He did a tomahawk, word-phrase-and-clause-dissection criticism on the poem, but was unhappy with himself and the resulting essay. That particular form of criticism he never tried again.

Generally, Thompson took just the opposite approach, and it worked almost as well. Although he praised almost everything — Southern and Northern — the generosity he showed to the South made the *Messenger* popular. It came naturally to him. Thompson was during the whole of his formative years a happy and successful young man in those things which were most important to him. He carried with him for most of his life a disposition to think the best of people and events. The survival of the *Messenger* for the last decade of his editorship is testimony to his optimistic character. Thompson liked people; he liked literature of most kinds; and, up to this point in his life, he enjoyed work. All of this is evident in his criticism.

Thompson also had some definite prejudices, as all men do. He preferred the South and supported whatever its authors produced that was not absolutely bad. Even when he could not use a work, Thompson was as gracious as possible. For example, in refusing a weak poem, he wrote Augustin Louis Taveau of Charleston:

My apologies are due to you for having so long deferred returning the MS of the "Hermit" about which you made inquiry in your letter of the 8th July. I now send it to you. There is good poetry in the effort, but it is quite unequal, I think, and the story is hardly worth the drapery you have thrown over it. This of course is mere editorial criticism, made frankly to yourself alone, and not *ex cathedra* to the world. It always gives me great pleasure to hear from you, and in the hope that it may not be long before you will resume the pen, I remain. . . . [5]

On the other hand, Thompson did not sacrifice the literary independence of the *Messenger* for the popularity that a more thoroughgoing sectionalism would have brought him. His intention from the beginning of his association with the magazine was to promote good literature, wherever he found it. Doubtless, his sagacity proved beneficial to several young writers, Northern and Southern, who might never have achieved as much as they did without the support of the most prestigious literary journal in the South. Among those young aspirants were Henry Timrod — and everything he wrote pleased Thompson — Paul Hamilton Hayne, Frank Stockton, J. E. Cooke, Donald Mitchell, G. W. Bagby, and Joseph E. Baldwin. The last three of these were humorists, and Thompson was particularly keen in seeing the talents of humorists. Humor was popular in the South generally, as well as with Thompson, who wrote some very witty items himself. Of Baldwin and the Southern humorists, of whom Mark Twain is the finest example, Thompson wrote:

In the departments of humour we think it can not be questioned that Southern writers have excelled. The Georgia Scenes of Longstreet, Major Jones's Courtship of [W. T.] Thompson and Simmon Suggs of Hooper, constitute an aggregate of fun, the like of which it would be difficult to find in our literature, and here we have a humorist who in our judgment, surpasses them all. . . . The drollery of the writer [Baldwin] is irresistible, but apart from that there are graces of style which belong peculiarly to him. [6]

Thompson's support was not always productive of good writers like Timrod, Hayne, Cooke and Baldwin. Yet the products of such lesser lights as James Barron Hope, Susan Talley, "Amie," Mrs.

Margaret J. Preston, Laurence Neville, Taveau, Julia Pleasant, and Thomas B. Bradley was often, if not always for its times, good reading. It often pleases today. To give the South its due, however, it must be admitted that the *Messenger,* throughout its life, printed little of impressive quality, and the Southern readers who bought Northern publications showed more discernment than Thompson credited to them.

"Amie," a lady of Richmond who remains unknown to this day, is a case in point. Miller, in writing of this period, thinks Thompson pleased no one but himself and her in printing so many of her items; but B. B. Minor, who followed the fortunes of the *Messenger* throughout its existence, thinks "Amie" improved with effort and practice. Writing of Thompson's last year as editor, Minor comments, "How Amie has expanded! Mr. Thompson might have made her Mrs. Editor."[7] But Thompson believed earnestly that support was more conducive to the great literary awakening — which he was sure the South was on the verge of experiencing — than was harsh criticism. Throughout his life he continued to urge the South to honor her poets, and he preached that Southern writers should use the material of their own lives and native country.

Thompson's support and praise was not confined to the South. Such a practice would have been contrary to his beliefs concerning the duties of a critic; foremost among these duties was to present with impartiality critical notice of new works and writers, even when such a practice means incurring hatred:

Yet, malgre, this embarrassing fact, he should remember, that a book is to be estimated of itself, that it must stand or fall by its own merits, and recognizing no personal consideration, he should come up manfully to the discharge of his critical labors.[8]

Nonetheless, when Thompson's criticism is seen in perspective, the impression is almost unmistakable that he "manfully discharged his critical labors" in making unfavorable comments on Northern writers just a little more than on Southern writers.

He did find much to praise among the volumes from the North. Above all, he praised Hawthorne, but somewhat at the expense of other Northerners:

A peculiar favorite, among the New England men of letters perhaps for reason that his literary fame has not been acquired by that system of friendly puffery to which most of these writers are indebted for their position. He has had no band of claquers to cry his writings into favor, but they have made their way by virtue of their own intrinsic merits. His reputation is therefore legitimate, and is not likely to be disturbed.[9]

He admired the moral tone of the writings and saw — somehow — Hawthorne as a "genial, receptive loving spirit — attuned to all that is good and beautiful in man and nature."

Such comments, which are numerous in Thompson's criticism, reflect another of his prejudices, but it was the prejudice of the Victorian world in which he lived and ostensibly, at least, of the South for which he wrote. I refer, of course, to the moral tag. Considering how sincerely Thompson responded to Longfellow's poetry — he liked in particular "Song of Life," "The Courtship of Miles Standish," and *Evangeline,* "All sweet stories, well told" — it is a little surprising that he should be even more impressed by the moody darkness of Hawthorne's ambivalent morality, but such was the case. He also had high praise for Melville, Bryant, and Holmes, whom he found gentle and playful, and, of course, his own protégé, Donald Mitchell, "Ik Marvel." His Southern proclivities allowed him to find few good points in Margaret Fuller, whose "most striking characteristic was devotion to human liberty, which sometimes reached excess of fanaticism."[10] Of course, the term, "fanatic," was used frequently by Thompson as a synonym for "abolitionist." Lowell, for example, was consistently viewed as a most ardent abolitionist and fanatic in whose works Thompson found almost nothing worthy of praise. He characterized "The Fable for Critics" as "loose, ill-conceived and feebly executed, as well in detail as in general." Certainly, there is some truth in such a criticism, however. Thompson's critical moralism was a constant in his writings, and whether a work was from North or South, England or the Continent, he never approved efforts which treated questionable morals or insinuated indelicate subjects.

Among the English writers whom Thompson praised was the poet laureate. But even Tennyson, that personification of the Victorian mind, came in for censure when he published "Maud." Once more Thompson voiced an opinion that proved popular both at home and abroad when he wrote of the poem:

If this extraordinary compound of mysticism and misanthropy had not appeared with the name of the English laureate on the title page, we should have been certain that it had its origin in one of two exceptional conditions of mind — either that of some unhappy lunatic — or that it was the production of someone who designed an attempt on the critics by endeavoring to palm off nonsense on them for profound philosophy.[11]

The Idylls of the King, however, with its overt Victorian morality, replete with chivalric trappings, Thompson praised ecstatically.

It is refreshing to turn and hear him sing once again of the old song of love and courtesy, of womanly affection and knightly trust. *The Idylls of the King* is a sweet strain, yet burdened with a deep humanity, and the music speaks rather of a certain mood of consciousness than to the ordinary sense of melody in forms of verse.... The flow of the blank verse is rather Shakespearian than Miltonic, that is, it resembles those exquisite passages in the plays of the great dramatist, in which he strikes the cords of love with such subduing sweetness, more than the organ bursts of the *Paradise Lost* on which the soul is lifted to "solemn adoration."[12]

Such comments reflect a great deal of Thompson's understanding of the role of the critic as a judge and guide toward those works which are morally and intellectually healthy.

For their moral values, and the power with which their ideals are expressed, Thompson singled out for particular notice the works of Carlyle and Macaulay. Of course, even before they met, Thompson was much impressed by Thackeray's *Vanity Fair.* Also he was in agreement with the majority of the reading public in praising the novels of Bulwer. Mere morality, however, was not enough to save a book which otherwise lacked literary merit, and Bulwer's *Harold* is an example. Thompson reviewed it without enthusiasm:

Its entire want of continuing interest is due perhaps to the intimate knowledge, all, who have read English history, possess of the incidents of the Saxon fall. We know everything in anticipation.... A romance of the same people and period, purely imaginative in design, would doubtless be far more agreeable a work.[13]

Clearly, it was not merely history he disliked in *Harold,* for he found much to praise in another historical work. Writing on the first volume of Macaulay's *History of England,* he said:

Written in a style, which may be regarded by some as rather too familiar for history, it is yet full of instruction, derived from an infinite variety of sources... and rendered probably more popular by that absence of dignity which had generally been regarded as one of the incidents essential to historical narrative....As we conceive this [depiction of the life of the masses] to be one of the greatest, if not the very greatest, of the objects of history, we must concede to the work of Mr. Macauley a very high character.[14]

Other qualities which Thompson valued in an author are revealed in his review of Thackeray's *Vanity Fair,* which appeared four years before the two met. Thompson draws a fine distinction between Thackeray's kind of satire and cynicism:

Yet our author is no cynic. If he makes war upon worldliness, he is not affected with misanthropy....We do not lay down one of Thackeray's novels, where we have encountered characters, (also too correctly portrayed,) of the worst description, with the impression on our minds that the world has it in nothing of goodness or purity. His terror of maudlin sentiment is such, that he even endeavors to cover his pathetic passages with playful irony. It is this very disposition, perhaps, that renders his pathos so exquisite.[15]

If it is not already apparent where Thompson finds the value of a literary work, he makes his point explicitly in reviewing *Les Confidences* of M. A. Lamartine in 1849. He charges the critic

To scan closely the moral of a book, and to ask in a true *cui bono* spirit, whether or not man is likely to profit by the publication of this, that or the other "remarkable work"...to consider whose soul may be enlightened whose heart gladdened by its perusal.[16]

Thompson's literary criticism is unoriginal and classic in its search for form and idea which have their origin in works already esteemed for having stood the scanning of generations. As a critic he looked backward and seemed often incapable of understanding the value of what was new in many works of genius. Moreover, he resented those which dramatized philosophical approaches which were contrary to his — and the popular — view of the way things should be. Of Emerson and the Transcendentalists, for example, he was intolerant and impatient, "Transcendentalism, so long as it keeps itself in the cloudy regions of metaphysics and moral sentiment, may escape confutation or exposure; you cannot *prove* its worthlessness, because you cannot bring it to any absolute and settled test."[17] He distrusted morbid psychology, bold experimentation, and overt egoism and failed to make some crucial distinctions — such as the distinction between the terror of Poe's tales and that of the German school. Most of these attitudes, which he may have postulated himself quite independent of influence, were commonplace enough among the magazine critics of the day. Foremost among those who probably did influence Thompson was N. P. Willis, editor of the New York *Home Journal.* C. G. Eggleston, writing of Thompson in his early days as editor of the *Messenger,* noted, "He was not yet fully grown up in mind. He sought to model himself, I think, upon his impressions of N. P. Willis...."[18]

Other influential figures with whom Thompson had close associations from the first year of his editorship were Richard Henry Stoddard, Edmund Clarence Stedman, Thoms Bailey Aldrich, and — to a lesser extent — Bayard Taylor. These four made up the nucleus of the New York literary force field known as the genteel tradition, much of the glory of which was reflected from the older Boston triumvirate of Lowell, Longfellow, and Holmes. Along with the characteristics already mentioned, Thompson shared with the genteel tradition the feeling that he was at ease as a writer only when in an established society, working within the rules of the entrenched class and praising only the forms and ideas acceptable to it. Careful not to disturb or deride conservative current practice, he exalted the reigning manner while ignoring the crudities, the passions, the economic forces and urges of the merchant class and of the vulgar readers of petty literature. He defended a way of life by ignoring the disagreeable elements opposed to it. He was happy and optimistic as long as the *status quo* was preserved. To support his air of refined romanticism, he laced his diction with phrases from French, German, Latin, and Greek. He bandied about intimately the names of the great in literary, political, and social circles. And he talked.

He talked endlessly about the poet and his craft, of periodicals and policies and publishers, of techniques and devices, of the role of the poet and of literature; and he praised most immodestly his friends, who in turn praised him in unabashed pufferies. Had Thompson been more closely associated with the well-settled and secure New York establishment — a thing he much desired and tried on several occasions to accomplish — he might have fallen in line with the genteel tradition even more firmly. As it was, Thompson was forced to deal with and admire the rough and crude humor of the Southwest humorists; nor was he ever so totally blind as the members of the genteel tradition to the claims of some of the younger writers. He did not view the Muse as a divine mistress in whose service he gladly suffered; nor did he adopt the attitude of the troubadour toward women, nor write plangent drivel over his dying sweetheart, nor constantly praise the theme of a sound mind in a sound body, the primitivist's pretense.[19] On the other hand, what Thompson did praise in agreement with the genteel tradition was not always petty; quite the contrary.

Unlike the genteel tradition, Thompson found great works among the writings of Poe, Simms, Timrod, and other Southerners. He also admired Twain, Baldwin, and Longstreet, all of whom were ignored by the Northern genteelists. Still, it would be hard to disagree with the general approbation of the great works of Emerson, Longfellow, Lowell, and Holmes — whose accomplishments include *Nature* (1836), *The American Scholar* (1837), *Essays, First and Second Series* (1841-1844), *Representative Men* (1850), *Voices of the Night* (1839), *Evangeline* (1847), *A Fable for Critics* (1848) — though few praised it much — *The Biglow Papers, First Series* (1848), *The Vision of Sir Launfel* (1848), *The Autocrat of the Breakfast Table* (1858), *The Professor at the Breakfast Table* (1860).

Finally, Thompson did not agree with the genteel tradition in its refusal to recognize change. In one of his best poetic efforts, for example, Thompson wrote:

> The world has changed — there are who gravely doubt
> If the great epics have not long died out —
> No more in grandeur the Homeric line
> Repeats the story of a Troy divine. . . .[20]

In this poem, "Poesy: An Essay in Rhyme," Thompson asserts the classic — rather than romantic — position and codifies one of his most consistent critical ideas. Whereas he regrets the passing of the golden Age, he is realist enough to see that, while his time is not a great age of poetry, there is a need to keep up the tradition so that it may in time be passed on to better poets. Nor does he completely scorn current products:

> But while the amaranth waits for kingly brows
> Some laurel wreaths our greatful love allows
> To him whose sunny genius lifts to light
> The meanest objects of our daily sight:
> . . . .

> And yet not long, oh Poesy, not long,
> May War, earth's oldest and its direst Wrong
> Demand they paeans — Mercy waits and pleads,
> With thee to celebrate *her* glorious deeds.

This last passage would certainly have set Thompson apart from his New York friends and their love of romantic adventure, as it separated him from the thinking of most Southerners.

In the closing line of his poetic essay, Thompson again laments the changing world of letters, though he hopes for a return to greatness:

> As age of iron follows age of gold,
> The dear illusion we would *not* resist
> Fades, like curtain of dissolving mist,
> Before the glare of science, reaching far
> From wave to mountain, and from star to star,
> And still dethroning, disenchanting fast
> The idols and the idylls of the Past.
> We'll not believe it.

Here, as elsewhere, while Thompson shows his love of much in art revered by the genteel tradition, he is practical and develops his own line of thought. Particularly is this true in the closing couplet in which he acknowledges the wide human involvement in poetry

> All, all are poets on whom God confers
> The gift of Nature's true interpreters.

During his years with the *Messenger,* and under the influence of the urban environment of Richmond, Thompson advanced also as a writer of *belles lettres.* Perhaps his greatest strides were in the informal essay, the form taken in many of the Editor's Table commentaries and the ill-fated *Across the Atlantic.* The Editor's Table, along with other occasional essays over the years, reveals a writer very much at ease in his knowledge of a wide variety of subjects, and one much influenced by the style of Charles Lamb. His subjects include travel, language, manners, dress, trees, and some remarkable for their oddness, as for example "The Theory of the Toilet." The numerous excerpts already quoted from this essay and others which appeared in the *Messenger* should provide sufficient example of Thompson's style as an essayist.

Thompson also developed as a poet, although he was never to be

a great poet. Yet poetry should perhaps be seen as a community en-
deavor, despite the proud claims of individualism of any one poet;
the great poets come only after the innumerable attempts of bad or
mediocre poets have worn bare the path from which the genius
departs. Such a path-follower was Thompson. He attempted
nothing new or original, but he had a broad genial and compassionate view of man which, if it did not inspire often moved his readers
to pity or laughter.

One of his strengths was in humorous poetry, which has never
been recognized as one of the higher forms of art. At his best
Thompson accomplished something close to the comic poetry of
Lord Byron. He was a poet in the classic mold of the occasional
poet; most of his pieces were inspired by or commemorative of a
significant event in his life or, often in the life of his community.
Such a work was his "Inauguration of the Equestrian Statue of
Washington, Richmond, Virginia, 22 February 1858. Opening
Ode." This stately "Ode" on Crawford's statue is representative of
the sort of poetry which earned him the honorary title of Richmond's laureate, although that title much predates this poem:

> Not queenly Athens from the breezy height
> 　　Where ivory Pallas stood,
> As flowed along her streets in vesture white
> 　　The choral multitude:
> Not regal Rome when wide her bugles rolled
> 　　From Tagus to Cathay,
> As the long triumph rich with Orient gold
> 　　Went up the Sacred Way;
> Not proud basilica or minster dim
> 　　Filled with War's glittering files,
> As battle fugue or corronation hymn
> 　　Swept through bannered aisles,
> Saw pageant, solemn grand, or gay to view
> 　　In moral so sublime,
> As this which seeks to crown with homage due
> 　　The foremost man of time.[21]

Another was occasioned by a visit to Brandon, the Byrd plantation, in the company of Edward Everett and others. Here in past
ages it had been a tradition for distinguished visitors to cut their
initials into the glass:

> As within the old mansion the holiday throng

> Reassembles in beauty and grace,
> And some eye looking out of the window by chance,
> These memorial records may trace
> How the past, like a swift-coming haze from the sea,
> In an instant surrounds us once more,
> While the shadowy figures of those we loved,
> All distinctly are seen on the shore.[22]

Another short poem shows him in a lighter mood, not unlike that of some of Whittier's better poems. It is called "The Picture":

> Across the narrow, dusty street
>   I see, at early dawn,
> A little girl, with glancing feet
>   As agile as a fawn.
> An hour or so, and forth she goes,
>   The school she brightly seeks,
> She carries in her hand a rose
>   And two upon her cheeks.[23]

Thompson also wrote a number of serious poems, such as his "Sonnet on the Death of Webster" and the "Dirge for the Funeral Solemnities of Zachary Taylor" and the "Phillip Pendleton Cooke" poem written on the death of his close friend. A few lines from the Taylor dirge are as good as any he had done of this type.

> Again the cold, insatiate grave
>   Has newly closed above the brave;
> Again in solemn form we meet
>   A chieftain's virtue to repeat
> Bedew with tears the laurel leaf,
>   And sing the low, sad dirge of grief.[24]

It is a solid, workmanlike, conventional poem, durable and at times touching, topical, appealing, and immediate. The value of unoriginal language is particularly evident in expressions of sorrow, when shock finds solace in the familiar; and for Thompson's readers anything more original would have been disturbing. It is, in short, competent magazine verse.

The humorous verse is nicely represented by his "Linden," inspired on his trip to Europe:

> Ah! when at last we there shall meet,

> A jolly dinner we shall eat,
> And every bottle 'neath our feet
> Shall tell of vanished Burgundy.[25]

Here obtrusive rhyme adds to the humor. Elsewhere, Thompson acknowledged the influence of Byron, as for example in "The Rhine," where he copied stanzas (numbers 48, 49 and 59 of Canto III) from *Childe Harold's Pilgrimage*. Another, longer sample of humorous verse is his ballad "A Legend of Barber-Y." Here are the first two stanzas:

> There was a little dandy man that lived — no matter where —
> Who thought it vastly *comme il faut* to cultivate his hair,
> And so he kept in constant pay a hair (and whisker) dresser —
> Who called himself in pompous phrase "tonsorial professor" —
> Beneath whose kindly curling-tongs our hero's ringlets twined,
> Not Absalom's so beauteous grew, not hung so low behind;
> And soon upon his upper lip, right wondrous to behold,
> There sprouts an immense moustache with sunny hue of gold.
>
> Along the street this dandy man would walk at set of sun,
> And as the ladies passed him by he'd throw at every one
> Such melting looks from underneath his hyacinthine curls
> That fixed forever was the fate of all those happy girls;
> In vain they tried to think no more of such ambrosial tresses.
> Night, with its hours of dreamy rest, but deepened their distresses.
> For in their visions soft and light Don Whiskerandos came,
> A halo round his shinging hair and his moustache in flame![26]

Yet, alas, for all his success — indeed because of it — poor Don Whiskerandos comes to a tragic end. It is a poem in good humor — and perhaps not without a note of self-consciousness and a bit of wishful thinking.

He acknowledged special admiration for Shelley, though he was not often capable of imitating Shelley in his own poetry. At times, he could turn a graceful phrase, but he lacked depth of thought and any mastery of subtle prosody. All of his poetry was characterized by the hackneyed and cumbersome poetic diction of the eighteenth century. This was evidently a matter of choice, for Thompson frankly resented the "bold lyrical" innovations of Tennyson's "Maud," and was even more offended by the "coarse diction" of Whitman.[28]

Thompson also tried his hand, from time to time, at translations of poetry from French and German. It is no mean art, and Thompson was generally considered quite good at it.

Up to this point, we have looked at Thompson's better poems. He was not always up to the examples here cited. For example, on the occasion of Jenny Lind's performance at Richmond, for which Thompson was responsible, he wrote a farewell verse:

> How shall we speak of that brief dream
>   That passed so quickly o'er us,
> Wherein we caught the radiant gleam
>   And heard the heavenly chorus.
>
> Awhile we walked adown the lawn
>   Of early, beauteous Eden,
> Or strayed at early break of dawn
>   Along the hills of Sweden.
>
> And when, next day, her coach and pair
>   Were to the depot driven
> We stood like Pilgrims at the Fair
>   When Faithful flew to heaven.
>
> Alas! the bird, indeed, has flown
>   On lightest, swiftest pinions,
> To seek a yet more sunny zone
>   Among the Carolinians.[29]

Its rhyme is regular; the allusion to Faithful of *Pilgrim's Progress* is well conceived, but the last quatrain, like most of the rest, is egregiously bad. It was intended only as a spur-of-the-moment compliment, of course. Certainly, his criticism, essays, and poems did not lower the standards of the *Messenger*. Nor would they have lowered the standards of any other American magazine of the 1840s and 1850s, for his weaknesses were characteristic of American prose and poetry as a whole at this time. With the possible exception of William Gilmore Simms, no man in the South did more to influence literary development.

CHAPTER 5

The War Years

A T age thirty-seven, Thompson arrived in Augusta, Georgia, on
May 18, 1860 — with his thirteen years as the editor of the
South's leading magazine behind him, his health poor, his loved
ones hundreds of miles away, a new journal with little reputation to
nurture and the tropical summers in a provincial little town to look
forward to. A week later he wrote to Kennedy:

I have been in Augusta now just eight days, have got fairly to work in my
new editorial chair, have seen something of society, and may speak (with
caution) of the impression that has been made upon me and the probabil-
ities of my liking the change I have carried out in my life. [Augusta is]. . .a
very stupid little provincial town, which I would not choose as a residence,
even for a sweetheart's sake. There are many fine residents here, and a refined and agreeable circle, but this poorly compensates me for the utter
stagnation which reigns around.... Think of Rome without its ruins,
Rome without its Coliseum or Baths of Caracalla or Borghese Villa, Rome
St. Peter's-less, Rome, as Gen'l Jackson said 'in Georgy', and fancy yourself a resident of the town for the summer months![1]

That Thompson was disposed to dislike Augusta, whatever it
might have been, is quite evident. He had always loved his home
city of Richmond, and for more than a year had entertained hopes
of moving to nearby (about one hundred and thirty miles) Baltimore. Suddenly, events had changed his entire expectation and future. Some part of his estrangement probably had to do with the
girl he left behind him. Thompson was always reticent about his interests in women, but we do have a hint of such an interest in the
phrase "even for a sweetheart's sake" in his letter to Kennedy. Also in a letter from J. E. Cooke of May 24, Thompson is urged,
"Get thee a wife!"[2] — which is an improbabe suggestion unless
Cooke had some expectation of Thompson's specific inclination in

that direction. Then, too, on the back of a letter to George W. Bagby, dated May 25, as was the letter to Kennedy, Thompson wrote, "I have heard nothing in reply to my last letter, from my fair friend."[3]

Another, very different consideration which made Thompson long to be in Richmond or Baltimore was the turbulent political situation. Thompson had remained out of politics for the most part, an attitude which doubtless would have changed had he stayed in Richmond, but which changed even more fundamentally now because he was surrounded by Georgia politics — strange names and attitudes — and it was almost the only topic of conversation. He was never to join the social circles of Augusta or ever think of himself as anything other than an outsider. This may have been due in large part to the inescapable political discussions. Almost willfully, therefore, he deprived himself of one of his greatest pleasures, that of polite conversation.

The Southern Field and Fireside had been conceived by James Gardner, editor of the Georgia *Constitutionalist* and owner of several large plantations. William W. Mann, hired as Thompson's Paris correspondent in 1847, was its first literary editor; Daniel Lee, M.D., was agricultural editor; and William N. White, horticultural editor. The latter two represented the "field" part of the magazine and Mann, the "fireside." Gardner's intention was to appeal to his rural neighbors through their interests in farming and thus expose them to literature; and Mann had carried out the plan well. Since his early days as a correspondent with the *Southern Literary Messenger,* Mann had gained throughout the nation a respected reputation as a man of sound taste. When the *Field and Fireside* was getting underway, Thompson had written:

We can truthfully say (and we feel an obligation to do so at this time) that in our judgment there is not in the United States a person more admirably fitted for the conduct of a literary journal than Mr. Mann.[4]

Dr. Lee was a Northerner who had made himself noticed, if not infamous, by publicly arguing against the right of secession; so Thompson had at least one ally on this point.

It was probably Mann who recommended that Thompson be hired as his replacement as literary editor of the weekly. That Thompson might accept was dependent on at least two things: more money and less work; but in addition it seems that Gardner

had also held out the possibility that Thompson might be allowed
to move the journal to Richmond, once it was fairly launched. The
money was much greater and the work was less: for each weekly
issue, he was to write a page of editorials and reviews and to com-
pile a serial, one or two informal essays, and a few poems from
other pens. For these works, Thompson appealed to his old friends
and contributors of the *Messenger* days. Now with a sufficient supply of money, he could pay for the best works available and no
longer had to fill the pages with inexpensive or free material. The
names and works of former *Messenger* contributors, therefore,
were frequent in the pages of the new magazine. John Esten Cooke,
William Gilmore Simms, Paul Hamilton Hayne, Julia Pleasants,
and Mary E. Bryan all appeared in the *Southern Field and Fireside,*
and were paid well and regularly.

Unfortunately, Augusta weather was more than Thompson had
expected. His consumptive condition was always irritated by hot
weather. Augusta, a popular winter resort because of its pleasant
weather, was hot and humid in summer and the lack of adequate
sanitation aggravated its unhealthy climate. Daily baths and "tem-
porate habits" kept Thompson going through May, when he wrote
to Kennedy: "As to the climate, this I confess, gives me some
anxiety. At this moment, in May, the heat is overpowering and I
have to keep within doors till near sunset. What it will be in dog
days, I shudder to think." [5] The summer of 1860, as a matter of
record, was unusually hot, and Thompson finally could not stand it
longer. His health failed, and he went back to Richmond in the
company of a doctor.

In August he wrote an editorial letter for the *Field and Fireside,*
and on the first of September he was again well enough to write an
editorial. That same week he visited New York with his mother,
then went on to Newport where he hoped to meet Kennedy. From
Newport he wrote again for the editorial section of the magazine.
After several weeks in Newport, his strength returned, and he was
back in Augusta in time for the October 13 issue of the journal. He
was unwilling, however, to remain there and asked Gardner to re-
lease him from his contract. Thompson resigned his chair to his assistant, who had been doing his job since July. In the issue of
November 17, Thompson wrote farewell to Augusta.

I cannot forbear offering my thanks to the press and public — nor can I
withhold a grateful acknowledgment of the personal kindness which has

been extended to me, a stranger, by the hospitable citizens of Augusta. For years a zealous though unworthy votary of letters, *in* the South and *for* the South, with every feeling and aspiration for the intellectual advancement for the Southern people among whom I was born, I cannot be indifferent to the future success of the *Field and Fireside.*[6]

He returned to Richmond and began looking for a job.

In the spring of 1860, before his stay in Georgia, he and John Cooke had begun a collaboration on a book of poems on the South at the request of a New York publisher. It was to this task that the two young writers now devoted themselves. Cooke was sure that the book would be profitable and had written to Augusta to encourage Thompson, "with the advent of early autumn we must put on double harness, and *toil* at the book. It will pay us *largely* and *steadily.*"[7] Their efforts were insufficient to meet the autumn deadline; but, granted an extension, they continued work on the collection well into January.

On January 9, 1861, Thompson went to New York, probably to deliver the manuscript or some part of it, for Van Moore of Schribner's was working on the manuscript of *The Poems and Poetry of the South* on into April.[8] Perhaps, too, Thompson was still seeking permanent employment. Unfortunately, he came down with a severe cold. Near the end of January, he started south again, stopping in Baltimore to visit the Kennedys. It was here that news reached him of the illness of his sister's husband, Henry W. Quarles. He arrived in Richmond too late to see his brother-in-law alive. He wrote to Kennedy, "I found a sad household. My sister Susan has been left in narrow circumstances, which fact in itself makes me exceedingly anxious to get to work at something." His anxiety stemmed from another quarter also; a month earlier he had written to the same man, "I have not the heart to say a word about public affairs. We are on the verge of civil war."[9]

War was in the air: business had slowed down; jobs were not to be had. Idle thousands roamed the streets, waiting for news. South Carolina had seceded in December of 1860, after Lincoln's election. In Richmond on January 7, newly inaugurated Governor Letcher called a special session of the state legislature to elect delegates to a state convention for the purpose of deciding the future of the Union. Thompson asked Kennedy to contact the *Baltimore American,* offering his services as the Richmond correspondent for the Convention. The Baltimore paper was not interested in the

Richmond Convention and remained, wrote Thompson with a show of bravado, "insensible to the claims of so brilliant a journalist." Kennedy remained his only Baltimore correspondent.

Depressed by the death of his brother-in-law and his own cheerless future, Thompson, nevertheless, followed the Convention closely. It was almost certain to make him heartsick. To Kennedy he gave his impressions of the first meeting:

There is an immense outside pressure of clamorous seccessionists who desire to carry the State out of the Union by intimidation, but it will not succeed. Yesterday the galleries were very properly cleared by the presiding officer, and last night an immense mob with music and banners went the round of the hotels serenading the *extreme gauche,* calling on the leading men for speeches, etc., etc. If anything like a reasonable adjustment is agreed upon at Washington, this convention will never adopt an Ordinance of Secession.[10]

The Peace Conference in Washington, to which Thompson alludes, did suggest a reasonable adjustment, but Congress did not act on it effectively. Already the Confederacy was organizing; Jefferson Davis headed the new government in Montgomery. Virginia, however, had not committed herself. Thompson prayed she would remain within the Union.

At about 4:30 A.M. on Friday, April 12, 1861, the guns at Fort Johnson began firing on Fort Sumter, near Charleston, S.C. The news reached Richmond amid great excitement. Rumors were flying. Business was suspended while the citizenry flocked about the newspaper offices. In the office of the *Richmond Whig,* a crowd had gathered around a large map of the Charleston Harbor on which battle positions were marked. At two o'clock the Stars and Stripes were lowered and a white flag replaced them. Celebration began in Charleston; a little later, in Richmond, extending into the night. Bonfires were lit, fireworks set off. Richmond's newspaper offices were ablaze with light — *The Enquirer,* Daniel's *Examiner,* and the *Dispatch* — except for the windows of the proUnionist *Richmond Whig,* which were as dark as the prospects in Thompson's heart. The Richmond Convention, however, was still divided.

Three days later, on April 15, Lincoln called for seventy-five thousand troops. On April 17, Virginia joined the Confederacy. Once Virginia had decided her course, Thompson no longer held any reservations. His way was clear, and he embraced it with the enthusiasm born of despair. Lincoln's call for troops had forced the issue. He wrote to Kennedy:

...That fatal document in an instant changed seventy-five thousand loyal friends of the Union into bitter enemies, and there is absolutely no division of sentiments among us now. All your old party and personal friends are fixed and resolute in their attitude of resistance to the hostile course of the administration....all unite in the so-called rebellion.[11]

For Thompson the certainty of war brought certainty of employment. His health made him unfit for military duty, but there was much to be done on the civilian front also. Sometime in the early months of the war Thompson became assistant to the Secretary of the Commonwealth of Virginia, Colonel George Wyth Munford, father of Thompson's friend "Billy" Munford. As Secretary of the Commonwealth, Munford was also State Librarian with offices in the Capitol building, and it was here that Thompson worked also during the first years of the War. Thompson was general factotum to Colonel Munford, doing both office and library work. He also issued the official war news — and in that capacity was press secretary to the governor, for whom he also served at times as a speech writer. From his office in the State Capitol atop Shockoe Hill, he would later have a commanding view of the camps around Richmond several miles away.

Thompson also spent much of his time writing, for there were now many demands for skillful writers, particularly those with connections in high places. Thompson had a number of such connections. His closest friend, John E. Cooke, became aide de camp to General J. E. B. Stuart. (Stuart himself was a close friend to Thompson.) His former employer, the Honorable James A. Seddon, would be named Secretary of War for the Confederacy. The entire journal and newspaper industry was familiar to Thompson, as was the Richmond society from whose ranks so many of the leaders of the rebellion would come. Added to all this, his record as a writer made Thompson a very salable property. The South was finally becoming interested in what writers had to say, even if this interest was largely restricted to news of the war. Still, a new interest in belles lettres began to develop also, especially in war poetry. Propaganda was the basic determination of most publications throughout the war, so governments North and South had a very considerable vested interest in all types of publications. Dr. George

Bagby editorialized in the April issue of the *Messenger*, "A great work is to be done.... A subject people are to be rescued from domination of fanatics; a new literature and new centres of trade are to be established."[12] Publishing became big business and new magazines and newspapers sprang up all over the nation. Richmond alone added five new publications during the early years of war, and Thompson had editorial connections with two of them.

Southern newspapers in the 1850s had been popular and well-written. Though the Northern literati had some justification in sneering at Southern productions in prose and verse and at the thinness of its literary magazines, the North did not enjoy any superiority in journalism. The best newspapers of the South ranked with the best of the North. George D. Printice of the *Louisville Journal,* George W. Kendell of the *New Orleans Picayune* and the *Mobile Register's* John Forsyth were editors with power and rhetorical gifts, dominant in shaping the mind of the South. Moreover, they invited essays and discussion from well-qualified spokesmen on diverse and controversial issues. In addition, they devoted considerable space to reprinting literary items. They were, in effect, literary magazines as well as voices of public opinion and reporters of events. The editor was often a "cross between statesman-politician and the man of letters." What he editorialized was usually more interesting to his readers than the news, which was normally national, until after the beginning of the War when national and local merged.[13]

In Richmond the leading newspapers at the beginning of the War were the *Whig,* the *Examiner,* the *Dispatch* and the *Enquirer* (the oldest of Southern newspapers, a semi-weekly founded in 1804). The *Sentinel* came later. Whitelaw Reid, a capable Northern journalist, wrote this of the Richmond press in 1866:

The newspapers of Richmond, throughout the war, were in many respects the ablest on the continent. Their writing was often turgid, but it was always effective; and it shaped the public sentiment of the whole Confederacy.... In the midst of their destitution they managed to keep up double the number of average dailies that we had in Washington, and the editorials of each were generally the productions of educated thinkers as well as red-hot partisans.[14]

Some years later Thompson and Reid would meet in New York and become fast friends.

Of the Richmond editors in 1861, none was more controversial, nor better known to Thompson, than the editor of the Richmond *Examiner,* John M. Daniel. He made the *Examiner* the "Ishmael of the Southern press, so far as it is against everybody." Thompson might have worked for Daniel, except that his political inclinations were nearer the philosophy of the *Whig* and his view of life generally was never, even in his darkest moments, as cynical and misanthropic as Daniel's. Be that as it may, Thompson's position as assistant to Colonel Munford may well have kept him from actively working for any of the Richmond papers as a reporter, at least during the first year.

Whatever Thompson's reasons for not associating with a Richmond newsaper, we do know that by August 1861 he was writing almost daily letters of war reports to the *Memphis Daily Appeal* under the pseudonym of "Dixie." The use of such covers — of not identifying the author at all — was a tradition of long standing. Before the war it was often a means of avoiding personal embarrassment. After the war began, the use of such names became a matter of great importance to the usefulness of the reporter. In a letter to George W. Bagby, Editor R. B. Rhett, Jr., of the *Charleston Mercury,* provides an illuminating example of anonymity among reporters:

I consider your connection with the Washington Correspondence as strictly confidential. No one in South Carolina, out of the *Mercury* office, knows your name; and if you will be discrate [*sic*] as I will, no one shall ever know. The wisdom and consequent usefulness of your letters will depend entirely upon this. If you are known, it is impossible to criticize and use names as you otherwise can do, to the great benefit of the Southern cause.

Crandell was my correspondent for some time, and was very useful in exposing the intrigues of sundry would-be fire-eaters at Washington until he, through impudence, allowed them to ferret him out. After that, he was of no account. Jones of New York has just been exposed, either through his own indiscretion, or the treachery of some telegraph operator — All this by way of caution.[15]

Such secrecy is readily understandable among the reporters who wrote correspondence from the North for Southern papers. They were in some cases looked upon as spies. However, much the same attitude was held by some officers and government officials toward the press in the South. There were, evidently, many personal foibles and governmental blunders to be hidden from newsmen. That Thompson was a correspondent for the *Memphis Appeal* was probably not known by any but his most trusted friends and relatives.

Throughout this time, Thompson was also writing occasional poems for newspapers and magazines. For the *Charleston Mercury* he wrote the first of his war poems, which shows how completely he had reversed his antiwar, antisecesionist views. In response to Lincoln's comments on government by force, Thompson wrote "Coercion":

> Who talks of Coercion? who dares to deny
>   A resolute people the right to be free?
> Let him blot out forever one star from the sky,
>   Or curb with his fetter the wave of the sea.
>
> Who prates of Coercion? can love be restored
>   To bosoms where only resentment may dwell?
> Can peace on earth be proclaimed by the sword,
>   Or good-will among men be established by shell?
>
> Once, Men of the North, we were brothers, and still,
>   Though brothers no more, we would gladly be friends;
> Nor join in a conflict accursed, that must fill
>   With ruin the country on which it descends.
>
> If, deaf as the adder itself to the cries,
>   When Wisdom, Humanity, Justice implore,
> You would have our proud eagle to feed on the eyes
>   Of those who have taught him so grandly to soar.
>
> And the bugle its echoes shall send through the past,
>   In the trenches of Yorktown to waken the slain;
> While the sod of King's Mountain shall heave at the blast,
>   And give up its heroes to glory again.[16]

It is a poem representative of the sentiment, vigor, and poetic standards of the times. Certainly, too, it shows something of the American genius for finding a ringing phrase to justify the "ideals" of its wars. In Thompson's own canon, it is superior in phrasing, clarity, and immediacy to almost anything he had written up to this time. What is unusual about the poem is the note of reconciliation and Virgilian sorrow that creeps in from time to time. It is a quality of Thompson's war poetry that distinguishes it from any other

American poet of his time.

As if his job as state librarian, press secretary and speech writer were not enough — in addition to writing poetry and daily reports to the *Memphis Appeal,* which sometimes ran to ten pages — Thompson also became the Richmond correspondent for the London *Index,* a frankly propagandistic newspaper published in London by Henry Hotze as the Confederate organ in England. Jefferson Davis was convinced that one great hope for the success of the Confederacy was to bring England to recognize the C.S.A. as a separate and sovereign nation and then to lend aid and even military support. All of this support, Davis felt, would be realized because England's factories needed the South's cotton. There were other elements in Davis's thinking, of course; but Davis seems to have been right in thinking that, while England had announced a national position of neutrality in all matters dealing with the American Civil War, the English people and government favored the South. Davis wished to take advantage of this partiality through the *Index.* Thompson's knowledge of England — brief though it was — and his diplomatic qualities as well as his contacts with the State and Confederate governments made him a natural choice for this job. Despite his poor health, Thompson seems to have done an impressive job at all of these undertakings. He was not one of the top three or four reporters in the South, perhaps only because of his position in Richmond and his uncertain health; he was not able to follow the armies and give the kind of on-the-spot coverage that was most respected, needed — and dangerous. However, J. Cutler Andrews makes this comment:

As the most important news center of the Confederacy after May 1861, [when the Confederate Capitol was relocated there] Richmond was host for the representatives of most of the important Confederate dailies. Perhaps the ablest and most frequently quoted of the Richmond correspondents of the Southern press were Louis J. Dupre of the *Knoxville Register,* John R. Thompson, the "Dixie" of the *Memphis Appeal,* Salem Dutcher of the Augusta *Constitution,* and George W. Bagby, who represented a number of different newspapers.[17]

Thompson's mode of operation as correspondent for the *Appeal* and the *Index* was much the same as most correspondents, except that Thompson was confined to Richmond and the nearby scenes. Richmond collected news from whatever source was at hand. Long after other Southern cities had been cut off from Northern newspapers, Richmond continued to receive papers from the North, some smuggled in. There were the official news releases from the governments — of which for Virginia Thompson had charge — but these were likely to be late and cautious and calculated to favor the government. Rumors were soaked up with insatiable thirst. One correspondent informed the New Orleans *Picayune,* "They get up rumors here about battles and results as readily as Yankees get up patents for machinery, and both are about equally valuable and reliable. This is the most difficult city [Richmond] I have been in to discriminate between truth and falsehood, and you must not be surprised at the groundless reports you sometimes receive by telegraph."[18] Rumors were not always reported as fact, and Thompson seems to have been unusually reliable in stating a rumor as a rumor and often in showing the falsity of rumors when he had the means. Correspondents' reports were also filled with opinion of the writers and those he had interviewed. These opinions often had to do with the fitness of military and political leaders. Jefferson Davis, for one, was much criticized by the Southern press, among whom none was more relentless than the Richmond *Examiner's* editor, John M. Daniel. Battles and battle scenes were endlessly mulled over, each incident and every detail closely scrutinized and alternative plans of actions pondered. The waterways, the number, size and type of buildings, hills, even rocks of a given battle were described. Thompson, for example, in a slow news period after the battle of Centerville in October 1861, described the town by night — its tents, campfires, and lanterns, bordered by blackness and having the appearance of a large city — and then compared it to the scene in daylight: "a long straggling street with dilapidated houses at considerable intervals, the roadways very much obstructed by rocks...camps all around, horses hitched to every rail of the tumble-down fences...small specimens of 'peculiar institution', other 'contraband of war' peddling chickens and chestnuts...."[19] All of this material — along with whatever interviews, however informal — were put together, often with remarkable skill, to make up the letters.

Occasional, colorful word portraits of important figures proved very popular. When Lee first appeared as field commander, Thompson introduced him to a curious Confederate audience who had little knowledge of the man on whom so many hopes were placed:

His life, since he assumed the chief command of the Virginia forces, has been a model of soldierly patience and energy and watchfulness. Six o'clock in the morning has seen him regularly enter his office, which, with rare exceptions he has not left, save at meal times, till eleven at night. A man of few words, of unvarying courtesy, but of a singularly cold and distant manner, he has kept his own counsels with more than the impenetrable secrecy of Louis Napoleon, and no one has dared to trifle with his time upon unimportant or frivolous missions. If the visitor had business, he was requested to state it in the briefest or most direct way; if he came through sheer curiosity to see the man, or converse with him idly about public affairs, Gen. Lee excused himself so promptly and coolly that he never ventured to call again.[20]

Here is another, more informal sample of Thompson's technique from his first letter of the *Appeal*. "...We have a rumor on the street today, which everybody is discussing, that President Davis had himself made propositions for peace to the reigning despotism at Washington. It came to your correspondent from a source entitled to great respect, but he does not state it as anything more than a general report, furnishing the present topic of conversation."[21] Thompson goes on to report other topics of conversation. Then, citing letters and documents taken from prisoners and dead Federal soldiers, he comments on the shocking language and devilish spirit found in them. He concludes:

And yet these were the people who were to teach us morality and civilization at the point of the bayonet, who were to carry on Mrs. Harriett Beecher Stowe's "religious war," and spread Dr. Tyng's Bibles to the Gulf of Mexico.

From Western Virginia we learn that the forces under Brigadier-General Henry A. Wise had been compelled to fall back upon Lewisburg, in the country of Greenbrier, in consequence of the advance of a federal column 25,000 strong....

We hear today that a small skirmish took place yesterday at Falls Church in which 1500 more federal prisoners have fallen into our hands. What to do with them will be a puzzling question, indeed.

The President has just moved into the house purchased for him on Clay Street. No announcement has yet been made of special evenings set apart for levees, and I trust there will be none. While the war lasts, this pomp and ceremony may be left to his apeship in the Whitehouse at Washington.[22]

Such dispatches were sent off almost daily and arrived in Memphis — later elsewhere — in about five days to a week, generally; but some letters did not appear until two weeks or more from the time they were dated. Probably, too, some never arrived.

Often dispatches showed wide discrepancies from one paper to the next. Reports of numbers of casualties were likely to vary greatly, depending upon the temperament of the reporters, and reporters sometimes responded to one another with acrimony or disgust. When New Orleans fell to the Union forces in late April 1862, the Richmond *Dispatch* was inclined to take it lightly, saying the loss had been anticipated. Thompson contradicted the assumption of the *Dispatch,* declaring, ". . . The public mind had already been prepared for no such thing. On the contrary, no event was considered more unlikely during the whole progress of this war than that New Orleans would fall into the hands of the enemy."[23]

Several qualities set off Thompson's style of reporting from that of most of his contemporaries. He was among the best informed reporters of the war, due largely to his contacts in Richmond and friends on the battle lines. His information often came to him in fragments and as rumors. When it was, therefore, necessary to make judgments on the validity and usefulness of the bits of data, he did that better than most. He was enthusiastic about the South, frankly showing his prejudice, but did not allow his partiality to lead him to make exaggerated claims. Thompson was also not quite so pressed for time as many of the battle-line reporters; consequently, he was not given to making wild guesses. He was fair in his treatment of Southern leaders, criticizing his friends when they erred — as Stuart did in the early days of his campaigns — or supporting those whom he personally disliked if they accomplished noteworthy feats. Thompson thus gained a reputation for reliability and truthfulness. He was also a better stylist than most Civil War reporters, given to sentimental and emotionally packed language; but Thompson often balanced such purple prose with terse, tight reporting. J. S. Patton wrote of him, "Thompson was a poet in journalism and something of a journalist in poetry."[24] Finally, no other reporter was so emotionally attached to and interested in Richmond, the center of government and the site of some of the war's most vicious, sustained, and strategically important fighting. Letters written for the *Appeal* and the *Index* present a short history of Richmond in the war which is both insightful and useful.

By 1861 Richmond had grown to a population of about forty thousand. It was the leading tobacco market in the state and something of a railroad center. It was also connected by canal to Lynch-burg and had a deepwater terminal on the James River. Its major industry before the war was flour milling. It also had several large iron foundries and manufactured cottons, woolen goods, and paper as well as tobacco. Richmond also covered about three-and-a-half square miles of beautiful hills, valleys, ravines, rivers, creeks and woods. It had many beautiful residences and public buildings, including a Capitol designed by Thomas Jefferson. The Capitol was surrounded by a park of eight acres in which was located the Crawford statue of Washington, and a band box where on balmy evenings bands played for the stolling, chatting citizens. South of the Capitol was the business center of town, the principal thor-oughfare of which was Main Street, where Thompson's father and late brother-in-law had their shops. At Tenth and Main, four blocks from the elder Thompson's hat store, was the Spotwood Hotel, the center of the business section and the place for talk, coffee and cigars.

By the spring of 1862, some fifteen thousand government em-ployees and adventurers had been added to the population. Every-thing was scarce; prices soared and lawlessness was rampant. A correspondent of the Pettersburg *Express* asserted, "I will not say that it is as hard for a poor man to live here, as it is for a camel to go through the eye of a needle, but I can say, without endangering my veracity, that the poor man who can live in Richmond need have no fear of starving upon any other portion of God's foot stool."[25] Despite the unfavorable conditions in the city and the equally unfavorable progress of the war, Thompson could report in March that the people were hopeful: "Our people have made up their minds to a long and wasting war.... Volunteers are pouring in from all quarters.... The new feeling seems to have infused something of energy even into the departments."[26]

Thompson was a member of the Richmond society. For him the doors of private homes were open, and during the first and part of the second year of the war there was much entertainment, many parties, and celebrations. A social group called the Mosaic Club sprang up to provide a cheering escape from the fears of war for what was known as the "quiet set." The club met most often in the home of the Barton Haxalls, where Miss Lucy Haxall — the object of Thompson's ardent affection in the late 1840s — "handsome, stylish and with mingled geniality and savoir faire," entertained the club members and such occasional guests as Gen. J. E. B. Stuart and his aide John Esten Cooke. Thompson was still an admirer of the vivacious Miss Haxall, but he was now one among many. It was to this group that Thompson read some of his best war poems and heard them "discussed with a frankness that sometimes made the hypersensitive little poet stare."[27] The club also produced plays for the distraction of members and social Richmond. They held charade parties, too, and collected money for charity. It is little wonder then that Thompson could continue to see the plight of Richmond as being less severe than those outside his sphere of social activity did. It was not to last, however. The early months of 1862 were the last gay times for Richmond for years to come.

As living conditions continued to deteriorate and war news worsened as General McClellan in May 1862, led a Federal force up the Peninsula, panic gripped the city. Thompson wrote the *Appeal,* telling about "groups of excited men at every corner; dense crowds before the bulletin boards of the newspaper offices; long lines of army wagons rattling over the clamorous pavements; here and there, an officer in a smart, fresh uniform, in strange juxtaposition and contrast with a knot of pallid, ragged soldiers whom the bright sun had tempted to stroll out of the hated hospital; couriers, covered with the dust of the road on broken down horses, in feeble gallop towards the War Department."[28]

When Lee did not allow McClellan to reach Richmond, Richmond responded with a lightness born of relief. Then the summer came with the oppressive heat so injurious to Thompson's consumptive lungs. He described the city from what was probably more his own listlessness than that of others: "except for wagons and the occasional movements of troops our streets are as dull as the broad dusty road that leads through a country court, and the bustling, active capital of three weeks ago seems, by some spell, to have been provincialized."[29]

Shortly after this, Stuart led a brilliantly successful cavalry raid, and Thompson was granted permission to observe the Confederate defenses along Nine-Mile Road. Riding over the desolate countryside, he could hear the random crack of cannon from distant Federal lines. He saw briefly the Confederate commander and also saw a reconnaissance group dispatched. He returned to Richmond and described his day for the *Appeal.*[30]

It was out of Stuart's daring raid that one of Thompson's most famous war poems grew. The story goes that Stuart lost only one man in his entire gallop around McClellan's army. This was

Captain William Latené of the Essex County Cavalry, who fell where the Brockenbrough and Newton plantations meet. The Captain's brother found the body and remained with it until the women of the plantation with their slaves provided him a horse and sent him to rejoin the army, promising to bury the Captain. The Rev. Mr. Caraway was sent for; but the Union pickets would not let him pass, so the service was conducted by the women. Thompson knew nothing of the incident until some two weeks later when he received a letter addressing him as "Uncle John" and signed "Lucy Ashton."[31] Who the real "Lucy" was Thompson never recorded, but he did as she requested and wrote a poem on the death of her fiancé. Tennyson later declared it to be the "most classical poem written on either side during the war,"[32] and William D. Washington made of the scene a painting which was much admired. It is a fair sample of Civil War poetry, a ballad in eight six-line stanzas. Here are the opening and closing stanzas:

> The combat raged not long, but ours the day;
>   And through the hosts that compassed us around
> Our little band rode proudly on its way,
>   Leaving one gallant comrade, gray-crowned,
> Unburied on the field he died to gain,
>   Single of all his men amid the hostile slain.
>   . . . .
> And when Virginia, leaning on her spear,
> Victrix et Vidua — the conflict done —
>   Shall raise her mailed hand to wipe the tear
> That starts, as she recalls each martyred son,
>   No prouder memory her breast shall sway
> Than thine, our early lost, Latané.[33]

Thompson thus received remarkable pieces of information from unexpected quarters. In this case it was due to his reputation as a poet, for some considered him the best of the Southern war poets. He also gained a powerful and influential new friend among the ranks of Richmond's visitors and reporters. This was Francis E. Lawley, generally considered the best of the war correspondents, who represented the *London Times,* generally considered the world's best newspaper. Lawley was sagacious, tactful, and a foreigner. For all these reasons — plus the fact that President Davis was interested in gaining the good opinion of England — Lawley was especially favored, allowed to go wherever he wished. Since his reports were for the London readers, he was given interviews denied to others. Thompson, however, was able to use some of his privileged information for the *Appeal*.[34]

Another of Thompson's friends, John M. Daniel, assigned his editorial duties to an assistant and became an aide to General A. P. Hill. He was with Hill in June at the battle of Gaines' Mill, where he received a wound that contributed to his death several years later. Daniel was one of the few Richmond newspaper men able to give a firsthand account of this battle, fought just eight miles from Richmond, for the battle area had been declared off-limits to reporters. Thompson was among the crowd that waited all day, listening anxiously to the rolling cannonade. He was struck by the irony of the orderly, well-dressed spectators imposed against the barbarous slaughter of war, of "delicate women, hearing with composure the loud, incessant roar of artillery from the batteries of an enemy whose energies were...bent...upon the reduction of their city," and "children gambling upon the grass and crying out with delight as the sudden, fitful, explosion of the shells strewed the horizon with meteors...."[35]

Prisoners taken after the battle began coming in. As Thompson watched from the crowds lining the streets, he thought they did not look like a beaten people. They "bore themselves with no little insolence, and despite their be-draggled and soiled condition made no mean appearance."[36] Clearly, the tales of cowardly men, paid by fanatic politicians to murder their brothers, were somewhat overstated. The Yankees were as bold and dedicated a group of fighting men as the Southern Cavaliers.

During the fall of that year, lawlessness and scarcities compounded the city's problems. Thompson told his readers that "the scanty supply of coal has already deprived us of gaslight in the streets and thoroughfares, and the dearth of provisions is attested in the almost fabulous prices of all articles of daily consumption."[37] Prices continued to rise through 1863; also, in early March a small riot took place over a shortage of bread. Thompson did not think it of much importance, referring to it as a "somewhat senseless panic." A month later another riot of much larger proportions occurred. Thompson again reported the event, but he denied that it was justified. However, the War Department censured the subject tightly. Thompson clearly could not tell all that he knew of the prices, but he did indicate something of Richmond's problems when he reported in May 1864, a complete halt to railroad travel in and out of Richmond. Indeed, not even private travel was permitted, for the government was confiscating all horses not being used to bring supplies to the city.[38] Another reporter, Alexander of the Savannah *Republican,* priced flour at two hundred and fifty dollars per barrel, meal fifty dollars per bushel, feed five dollars per pound, and bacon seven to eight dollars.[39]

If Thompson was indifferent to the bread riots of March 1863, it may well have been because he had his mind on other things, for on March 17, 1863, his mother died. In January of 1864, he began to keep a diary of his war years. On March 17, he wrote, "Anniversary of my mother's death. May I take to heart the lesson of her blameless life, her sweet Christian graces!" May 12 he recorded another death: "Genl. J. E. B. Stuart died at 8 o'clock P. M. at the house of Dr. Brewer on Grace Street in this City."[40]

Andrews writes in *The South Reports the Civil War* of the events following Stuart's death.

The friendship of the newspaper man John R. Thompson with Stuart had been long; at the time of Stuart's death a handsome gift which Thompson had ordered for him from England was on its way to Richmond. A poem Thompson wrote in connection with Stuart's funeral and which was published in the *Richmond Examiner,* made a strong impression on Stuart's friends and admirers. On the morning the poem appeared in print Attorney General George Davis came into an informal meeting of the cabinet with a copy of the newspaper in hand.

"Gentlemen, have you seen the *Examiner* this morning?" he asked.

"No," was the reply. "What does it contain? Anything particularly savage against the Administration?"

The attorney general answered by reading the poem, which inspired exclamations of delight from the president's advisers.[41]

While Thompson stayed in Richmond, doggedly refusing to leave though his health had once more reached a very dangerous state, he continued to write for the Memphis *Appeal,* which did not stay in Memphis. Its story is certainly an interesting one, worth adding to our brief history of Civil War reporting in the South.

When Memphis seemed about to fall to advancing Federal troops in June of 1862, the proprietors of the *Appeal,* John R. McClanahan and Benjamin Dill, packed up their press, a "clinking one cylinder press with its wood burning boiler," and moved to Granada, Mississippi. Here they stayed until November 29, 1862, when once again the advance of the Union forces and their determination not to become an occupation press forced them to move farther south to Jackson, Mississippi. Here they pledged, as visitors, to avoid state politics and affirmed their intention to keep the *Appeal* alive.

Jackson, however, was only forty miles from Vicksburg, and Grant's army, in an attempt to cut off the river approach to Vicksburg, headed toward Jackson. The *Appeal* barely escaped capture, printing its last issue in Jackson on the morning of May 14, the same day Grant's forces entered the city. As Grant's men were on the way in, the *Appeal* — editors, supplies, and equipment — was on its way out. One of the pressmen recalled the event in later years:

We crossed Pearl River in a flat with our mules, and had just made the trip when the blue coats reached the other bank. They had nothing to cross on so they took it out in cussin us, and we gave them as good as they sent. . . . We cut the flat loose and she went sailing down to the Gulf, and then they cussed some more and we mounted our mules and rode to Brandon, where all the truck had been carried.[42]

They stopped in Meridan, Mississippi, to issue one small paper. Then they traveled by rail and river by Mobile and Montgomery, Alabama, to Atlanta, where on June 6, 1863, they printed the first Atlanta edition of the *Memphis Daily Appeal*. Finally, after Lee's surrender, they were captured near Columbus, Georgia.

While he was writing for the *Appeal,* Thompson also edited two new journals in Richmond. In the summer of 1862, he accepted an offer to work with the *Southern Illustrated News*. The proprietors, Ayers and Wade, wished to have Thompson both submit articles and give general approval of articles from others, while the proprietors remained at least titular editors. Thompson was also to attract the best writers possible, which he was able to do because the pay was good and Northern magazines were no longer open to most Southern writers. Simms, Hayne, and Timrod were among the best-known contributors to the *Illustrated;* so too were Bagby, Cooke, and young McCabe. Sometime during the summer of 1863, Thompson became its editor in fact as well as in deed. Simms wrote from Charleston: "I am really very glad to see that you have been translated to the editorial chair of the *News.* Your fine taste and ample knowledge of the history of literature will enable you to do for that work what is very much needed."[43] After this time,

Thompson wrote the weekly editorial, and probably some of the sketches of Confederate generals which appeared on the front of each issue. The *News* managed to stave off its financial troubles until after Thompson left it, but it expired at the end of 1864.[44]

In 1863, Thompson took on yet another job. This one was with the newly established Richmond *Record,* published by the West and Johnson Publishing Company. This, too, was a weekly, "devoted...to a brief and abstract chronicle of the time." The editorship of the *Record* was also not publicized, but letters between Thompson, Simms and General Henry W. Hilliard credit Thompson with functioning as editor. It was a journal of broad interests, touching on literature, war, Congress, business, and a "resume of foreign literature." Little original material was used. Thompson printed state papers, which were much in demand, and he selected articles and excerpts from foreign publications for reprint. This journal lasted only six months and ceased publication on December 10, 1863.[45]

Another of Thompson's remarkable attempts to publish in book form also occurred in 1862. In the *Southern Literary Messenger* for January, 1862, appeared the following notice:

Prof. Chase and Jno. R. Thompson, Esq. of Richmond, have undertaken the worthy task of rescuing from newspaper oblivion, the many excellent little poems which the war has called forth.[46]

Thompson wrote to most of the known poets of the South, but received less than he had hoped for. Nevertheless, he collected the poems, mostly his own and Timrod's, wrote an introduction, and sent it off to an English firm for publication. Apparently, the manuscript was lost at sea, perhaps captured by the Yankee blockade. It was never recovered, never published.

During the war years his own poetry showed improvement; but war poetry, by and large is not a type thought to rank among the greatest. Still, where human emotions are involved in struggles that transcend merely temporary prejudices, the possibility of good poetry is always in the offing. Thompson was probably right, however, when he proposed before the war that conflict is "eminently pernicious to the graces of literature." For this very reason, Thompson's most acclaimed poems at the time of their production have ceased to interest us. We do not believe in their inflated rhetoric or their empty bombast. "The Burial of Latané" is a case in point. Thompson wrote for a Richmond audience — those who had great interest in what was happening there — about an archetypal young soldier killed in battle; but the emphasis is on the particular time and place, not on the commonality of the human experience. Also, his much respected dirge "Ashby," like the great majority of war poems, once the intense emotional charge is relaxed, becomes less interesting. The second and fifth stanzas, the best, suggest the heroic concepts of war — romantic, cavalier, classical — that were still nourished in 1862:

> Well they learned, whose hands have slain him,
>   Braver, knightlier foe,
> Never fought 'gainst Moor or Paynim —
>   Rode at Templestowe:
> With a mien how high and joyous,
>   'Gainst the hordes that would destroy us
>   Went he forth, we know.
>   . . . .
> Then, throughout the coming ages,
>   When his sword is rust,
> And his deeds in classic pages —
>   Mindful of her trust —
> Shall VIRGINIA, bending lowly,
>   Still a ceaseless vigil holy
>   Keep above his dust![47]

"Dulce et decorum est pro patria mori — the old lie" was a bright truth. Still, in 1922 Allan Nevins could claim for Thompson some popularity: "Ashby, 'The Burial of Latané,' and 'Lee to the Rear' are known by every Southern schoolboy, while 'Music in Camp' is in every anthology of historical verse."[48]

Thompson rose above the average, and all of his native instincts to resist war, to see it as the barbarous thing it is, asserted themselves in two distinct ways. For all of the trappings of heroic bloodthirst to be found in poems on the deaths of his friends, Thompson seldom, if ever, wrote the kind of simpleminded call to destroy, to hate, to kill that so often characterizes the deep sincerity of war poets. His sincere poems are laments on the deaths of good men. Secondly, Thompson asserted his essentially civilized nature through poems of reconciliation, which came much earlier in Thompson's body of war poetry than it did in the poetry of his contemporaries. "The Battle Rainbow," written in 1862, is based on an occurance just before the Seven Days' Battle near Richmond. When Thompson viewed the battle grounds the evening before Hill's advance, he was struck with the appearance of a rainbow spanning the line of the Confederate camp. He went home that night to his Leigh Street address, wrote the poem, and sent it to a lady who had seen the rainbow with him and remarked on it as an omen of good luck:

> Then a long week of glory and agony came —
>   Of mute supplication and yearning and dread;
> When day unto day gave the record of fame,
>   And night unto night gave the list of its dead.
>
> Not yet, oh, not yet, as a sign of release,
>   Had the Lord set in mercy his bow in the cloud;
> Nor yet had the Comforter whispered of peace
>   To the hearts that around us lay bleeding and bowed.
>
> But the promise was given. . . the beautiful arc,
>   With its brilliant confusion of colors, that spanned
> The sky on that exquisite eve, was the mark
>   Of the Infinite Love overreaching the Land. . .
>
> And that Love, shining richly and full as the day,
>   Through the tear-drops that moisten each martyr's proud pall,
> On the gloom of the past the bright bow shall display
>   Of Freedom, Peace, Victory, bent over all.[49]

Another such sentimental poem is his little ballad "Music in Camp." On this occasion the Yankee and Rebel camps were on opposite sides of a river. As evening fell, a Yankee band began playing.

> Down flocked the soldiers to the banks
>   Till, margined by its pebbles,
> One wooded shore was blue with 'Yanks,'
>   And one was gray with 'Rebels.'
>
> Then all was still and then the band,
>   With movement light and tricksy,
> Made stream and forest hill and stand
>   Reverberate with 'Dixie.'

Again a pause, and then again
    The trumpets pealed sonorous,
And 'Yankee Doodle' was the strain
    To which the shore gave chorus.

And yet once more the bugle sang
    Above the stormy riot;
No shout upon the evening rang —
    There reigned a holy quiet.

No unresponsive soul heard
    That plaintive note's appealing
So deeply 'Home, Sweet Home,' had stirred
    The hidden founts of feeling.

And fair the form of Music shines,
    The bright, celestial creature,
Who still 'mid War's embattled lines
    Gave this one touch of Nature.[50]

Still another escape from war was to treat it humorously, and
Thompson wrote a number of comic poems, including "England's
Neutrality," a mock Parliamentary debate; "The Devil's Delight,"
in much the same vein; "Farewell to Pope," "Richmond's a Hard
Road to Travel," and "On to Richmond," after Southey's "March
to Moscow." They were good fun for the Mosaic Club and his
Confederate readers. A sample from "Old Abe's Message, July 4,
1861" shows Thompson exercising his journalistic talents in verse:

Herewith I beg to submit the report
of Butler, the general, concerning the sport
They had at 'Great Bethel' near Fortress Monroe,
With him and Magruder some four weeks ago;
And here, let me say, a more reckless intruder
For he's taken the "Comfort" away from Old Point,
And thrown our peninsula plans out of joint;
While, in matters of warfare, to him General Butler
Would scarcely be thought worthy to act as a sutler,
And that insolent Rebel will call to our faces
The flight at 'Great Bethel' the 'New Market Races';
Then supersede Butler at once with whoever
Can drive this Magruder clean into the river;
I shall be confident still to assert,
That the panic's fictitious and nobody's hurt.[51]

June of 1864 in many ways concluded Thompson's life in Richmond — and eighteen years of his adult life. Some fifteen of those years he had spent as an editor. The last five had been physically, mentally, and emotionally depleting. The winter of 1864 had been the worst in decades, the summer of 1863 had been unusually hot, and the summer of 1864 promised more of the same. Thompson had worked hard in keeping up with the demands of his job as assistant secretary of Virginia, as correspondent to the *Appeal* and the London *Index,* and as editor of the *Southern Illustrated News.* He was still active in church, social, and civic affairs, as his diary indicates. On March 13, 1864, he wrote, "Attended St. Paul's, Large number of leading Confederate officers at Church in the morning — General R. E. Lee, Longstreet, Bragg, Hood, McLaws, Whiting and others." That evening he "...dined with President Davis." In 1863 along with his other obligations, he also edited the *Record* and compiled the book of war verse. In addition, because of the immediate threat of Federal invasion of Richmond and the generally unpromising events of the war, every man in Richmond, regardless of health or age, was forced to take up arms, drill, practice, and stand guard duty. Such labor, Thompson could not stand. We do not know how much time he put in as a home guard, but George Bagby speaks of the eighteen-pound musket which he carried on guard duty. If Thompson had a similar weapon and was required to "march gracious knows how many miles, under this scorching sun," as Bagby describes it, he could not have lasted long. Already, in the fall of 1863, his tuberculosis had been reactivated, and his condition was serious. Cooler weather helped some, but he was still under a doctor's care and tired easily in the following spring. His friends recognized the inevitable conclusion to expect if he stayed in Richmond for the coming summer.

Thompson himself was convinced that he should go to London and join the Confederates who were already there, working to popularize the Southern cause. On June 20, he drew his last pay as assistant secretary of the Commonwealth and started his trip towards London. In his diary he wrote, "The hour of parting from family and friends for an indefinite period of time comes rapidly, and feeble health conspires with the moral emotion to make me exceeding wretched."[52] He had to be carried to the depot in Richmond and lifted by friends onto the train. His nephew, Charles Quarles, then accompanied him to Wilmington, North Carolina, from which he finally sailed on July 4 on board the *Edith,* which successfully passed the Federal blockade to Bermuda.

On July 8 he noted in his diary: "Dense fog off the coast. Lay in the trough of the sea, firing signal guns. Pilot came along and took us into harbor. Heard of the loss of the *Alabama* in the fight with the *Kearsarge.*

"July 22, Sailed from Halifax in the *Asia.* Crowded with passengers.

"August 3, London. Moved my luggage from Exerter Hill Hotel to 17 Saville Row, the old residence of [Richard Brinsley] Seridan, where he died."[53]

CHAPTER 6

London and New York

THOMPSON'S purpose in England was, first, to regain his health and then to join the staff of the London *Index*. On August 4 he paid his respects to the Special Commissioner of the Confederate States of America to the Continent at Large.[1] This was James M. Mason, who invited him to return that evening for dinner. Here he met Captain J. D. Bulloch of Georgia, Walker Fearn of Mobile, Alabama, and Alexander Collis and a Mr. Bulloch of Maryland. He was forthwith invited to join Mr. Mason and his secretary, James E. Macfarland,[2] and Alexander Collis on a trip to the Hebrides Islands, north of Scotland, and back by way of Ireland. In Scotland he visited Abbotsford and the Dryburgh Abbey, where he saw the original manuscript of Waverly. On August 31, when they arrived in Ireland, the party was welcomed to Knocklofty, the seat of the Earl of Donoughmore, where they were warmly greeted by the Earl, one of the South's staunchest supporters on that side of the Atlantic. The Tipperary Archery Club was being entertained at the time, and the Mason group was invited to join in the party. "Collation, band of music, profuse champagne. Ball in the library room, the country aristocracy present," Thompson wrote in his diary.

September 3 — Went with Mr. Mason to the Clonmel Club: cricket-match with the 10th Hussars... the regimental band played "Dixie" for us, and the officers received us most handsomely....
September 5 — Played croquet with the children. Took a long walk to gather mushrooms....
September 6 — Made a mint-julep for the company, which was much enjoyed. Oddest people in Clonmel, — beggars, street-singers, barefoot market-women with donkeys, hundreds of ragged children.[3]

On September 11, Thompson was back in London. The sea voyage, which took a month, and the trip to the Hebrides and Ireland, which took another month, seem to have restored him to good health. He was now eager to get to work with the *Index.* Henry Hotze, whom Thompson had known as a war correspondent in Richmond, was in charge of the weekly, and J. P. Hopkins did much of the editorial work. Thompson was known personally to Hotze, and to the readers of the *Index* his letters from Richmond had already served to introduce his mind and interests. Some twenty-five letters from Richmond had eluded the blockade and been published. He needed no further introduction to the staff and readers. Almost at once he began writing a majority of the three pages of editorials, the "Notes on American News," and sketches of Southern life.

His work was never identified in print, for great secrecy was maintained on all matters pertaining to supporters of the paper and its contributors. It is only from internal evidence and notations in his diary that any of the work can be identified as Thompson's. Also occasional letters, such as the one from his sister, Mrs. Quarles, dated July 2, 1865, identified his essays, in this case, "Richmond before the War." The first several weeks he was exceedingly busy at the *Index* office in Bouverie Street, putting out sixteen pages weekly. He was probably as happy as he could be in a time of war when his family and home were under imminent danger of destruction. He was intensely interested in his work, well paid and well entertained. After he had gotten the "run of things," his work settled into a routine. The first four days of each week were devoted to editorials and sketches for the *Index;* the remaining three days were his own to spend on miscellaneous writing, social engagements, and short trips.

The purpose of the *Index* was made clear to its readers with each issue, for a declaration of purpose was always reprinted:

The Index was established in May 1861, in the darkest hour of the Confederate fortunes, by earnest friends of Southern Independence, with the distinctly expressed object of being the representative in English journalism, of a gallant and struggling people appealing to the world not only for political, but still more for moral recognition. Since accepting this great trust *The Index* has unceasingly labored, by the combined aid of English and of Southern writers, to enlarge and extend the common ground upon which two nations could cordially meet, which need only to understand each other in order to cherish the warmest mutual appreciation and lasting friendship. The chief, and almost the sole difficulty has been, and is still, the callous indifference of the British Government on the one hand, and, on the other, the perplexity, to the Eruopean mind, of the unsolved and unprecedented problems involved in the management and education of four millions of the African race, intermingled with a population of the highest Caucasian type. This difficulty could be met only by a liberal fairness to every shade of honest opinion, by an inflexible adherence to truth under all circumstances, and by a bold avowal of convictions, even though ill-received. *The Index* does not claim to be neutral, but it claims to be independent in the highest sense of the word. It is because it must reflect and appeal to, at one and the same time, the public opinion of two countries as yet only imperfectly acquainted that this somewhat unusual description is called for.[4]

With these goals in mind *The Index* printed letters and essays from individuals and culled from magazines and newspapers from all parts of America. It served to inform the Southern colony in Europe and to influence sympathizers.

Thompson may have been chosen for this position as well for his writing ability as for his well-known and respected diplomatic ability. The nonliterary requirement of his position was that he meet the English people and make popular his cause by being popular himself. Most of the Confederates made this their own duty. Captain Walker Fearn joined Thompson in some of these social activities, which took up Thompson's evenings in a manner which was much to his taste, as many entries in his diary show:

September 26 — Left cards at Sir Edward Bulwer's, and on Robert Lytton, Owen Meredith.
Oct. 6 — Dined at Lady Georgianna Fane's.
Oct. 7 — Dined at Captainly Blakeley's, inventor of the celebrated gun. Charming dinner; immense block of ice in the centre of the table to keep the air cool; beautiful flowers, and dinner *a la Russe.*
Oct. 8 — Saw at Palgrave's a copy of first edition of "Idyls of the King," the whole edition of which was suppressed.
Oct. 11 — Lunched with the Countess of Harrington. Afterwards drove to a famous jeweller's in Regent Street, where we saw diamonds of the dowager Countess Cleveland, eight thousand pounds in value. They were for sale. Commenced a leader for the *Index.*[5]

Perhaps the most enjoyable, and in a way the most successful, of his social conquests was in the battle waged with Ralph Waldo Emerson for the support of Thomas Carlyle. With respect to Emer-

son, it must be acknowledged that Thompson was in London
whereas Emerson was in America, trying to win Carlyle's sympathy
by mail. On the other hand, Emerson had cherished his friendship
with Carlyle since 1833. Each agreed to disagree. Carlyle's sympathies were probably already with the Southern states, even before
he met Thompson. It was through his good friend, Anne
Thackeray, whose father had died in 1863, that Thompson met the
"Sage of Chelsea."

Captain Fearn had already made an attempt to gain an interview
with Carlyle which had been very ill-received. Miss Thackeray
intervened and arranged a meeting. "Only," she wrote Thompson,
"when you call, Mr. Carlyle will not take either you or Captain
Fearn for the dreadful sounding characters he mentioned in his
note."[6] So it was that Thompson had the pleasure of recording,
"Called with Fearn on the Misses Thackeray and drove afterwards
to Chelsea to see Thomas Carlyle. He was just going out and
desired us to come some evening, when he would be at home."[7] On
October 14 he and Fearn called again.

Drank tea and spent the evening with Thomas Carlyle at 5 Cheyne Row.
Mrs. Carlyle for some time has been an invalid, but made her appearance.
Lady Ashburton and Miss Baring came in after tea. He ran off into table-
talk about tea and coffee, told us that he had found in Lord Russell's
"Memoirs of Moore," which he called a rubbishy book, the origin of the
word *biggin:* it comes from one Biggin, a tinner. . . .Mr. Carlyle inquired
about the Confederacy, its resources, army, its supplies and food and
powder. He read a letter from Emerson, in which the Yankee philosopher
declared that the struggle now going on was the battle of humanity. When
we rose to say good-night, he called a servant for his coat and boots (he received us in dressing-gown and slippers), and walked us within a stone's
throw of Grosvenor Hotel, two miles, at half-past eleven! On the way
passing Chelsea Hospital, he burst into a tribute to Wren, the architect, of
whom he said there was rare harmony, a sweet veracity, in all his work.
We mentioned Tennyson, and he spoke with great affection of him, but
thought him inferior to Burns: he had known "Alfred" for years; he said
he used to come in hob-nailed shoes and rough coat, to blow a cloud with
him. Carlyle said he thought Mill's book on Liberty the greatest nonsense
he ever read, and spoke dispairingly of the future of great Britain; too
much money would be the ruin of the land.[8]

On November 16 Thompson again called on Carlyle: "At
Carlyle's who made many inquiries about Lee, whom he greatly ad-
mires. He talked brilliantly; spoke disparagingly of Napier and

other English historians, — said they knew nothing of war as an art.''⁹

Apparently, Thompson's efforts were somewhat successful with Carlyle. Thompson certainly demonstrated that he knew how to listen. But then the temperament of England generally seems to have favored the South. In September of 1864 the English supporters of the South had united the several widespread Southern Independence Associations of the British Isles into a national association, electing the Right Honorable Lord Wharncliffe as president and Thomas Hornby Birley as chairman of the Executive Committee. Shortly thereafter, on October 20, Thompson lunched with Lord Wharncliffe. Later, at Mr. Laird's, he met a large company of Southerners and English supporters. Among these was his old friend from Richmond, Commander Matthew Fontaine Maury. The most prominent of the native supporters were a Mr. Connolly, an Irish member of Parliament, and A. J. Baresford Hope, whose writing on the American War was widely influential.

Christmas that first year in England was a highlight of Thompson's social activities. He had travelled to Calais with General George W. Randolph and his wife, neighbors of Thompson in London, where they inspected the Hotel Dessein, now a museum, made famous by Sterne and Thackeray. They journeyed on to Paris where, after leaving the Randolphs at the Grand Hotel, Thompson was welcomed to the city by Charles Welch, at whose apartment on the Avenue Gabriel Thompson stayed. He visited the cathedrals, drove out to Bois du Boulogne, skated on a small lake, went to the Longchamps racecourse, saw members of the french *demi-monde,* and enjoyed dinners and parties. For New Year's Day he wrote in his diary:

Jan. 1, 1865, Paris — Took a cab and went to dine at Mr. Corbin's Rue de Varennes, Faubourg St. Germain Streets coated with ice. Mr. Corbin lives in magnificant style. The guests were Mr. Slidell, General Randolph, Commodore Barron, and a son of Commodore Stewart of the old United States navy. The dark day was in accordance with the feelings of Confederates in Paris. The new year opens in sorrow. May it close in joy! God grant it!¹⁰

The new year did not bring good news. On January 7, he heard of the occupation of Savannah by Sherman's army; on January 30, the capture of Fort Fisher. Then on February 15, word reached England that peace negotiations with Lincoln had been broken off. Thompson also recorded his impressions of London at this time:

Feb. 13 — In my walks about London I am painfully impressed with the majority, even in quarters not the worst. Streets are dirty, houses mean, the vast masses exhibit squalor, laboring classes never seem to wash. Children swarm everywhere. Fifty yards from Regent Street there are slums like Five Points in New York.

Feb. 23 — Paid a shilling for a stand on the top of an ale house to see the funeral procession of Cardinal Wiseman. The most degraded concourse of people I ever saw. Women bearing the marks of their husbands' brutality, boys and girls old in suffering and vice, ragged, debauched creatures.[11]

A short distance away, in the British Museum, Kark Marx was writing *Das Kapital* (published 1867).

Feb. 25 — Drove to the seat of Mowbray Morris, editor-in-chief of the London *Times*. A charming English house. My room very luxurious. *Cuisine* excellent, wines delicious. Could not help thinking of my father and sister at home as I ate and drank. Music and tea in the drawing-room, afterwards billiards, cigars, brandy and seltzer. In the morning visited stables, dairy, farm-yard, greenhouses, and conservatories. Mr. Morris was little disposed to discuss the war, except from a military point of view.

A month later, Hotze had informed him that the *Index* was bankrupt and would probably be discontinued in two or three months, Sheridan had defeated Early, and he had met an Englishman with Northern sympathies, "a rare thing." Yet Thompson keeping up appearances was still meeting famous personalities:

March 25 — Went to see Lady Donoughmore attired for a drawing-room at St. James's. The court being in mourning, only white was worn. Her dress was white illusion looped with pearls, white satin skirt and train, tiara of diamonds, superb necklace and bracelets of diamonds. The "lower class" gathered about the door to see the blazing liveries. Met Dr. Rae, the Arctic explorer, at Mr. Lewis's on Camden Hill: free-and-easy, incessant smoking, abundant ale and oysters. Woolner, Maillais, Lord Houghton, Holman Hunt, Duke of Sutherland, and others present. Tyrone Power's son sang capitally.

Then on April 15 he received news of the capture of Richmond. A little more than a week later, his sister wrote to describe the fire and evacuation of Richmond. His father's store and all its goods, his own library with all his books — all were burned. Then, surrender at Appomattox Court House. He wrote:

April 26 — Went to the Strand and remained all day writing on the *Index*. About two o'clock the editor of *The Standard* [Captain Humber] came in, bringing the startling news of Lincoln's assassination on the night of the fourteenth in the theatre at Washington by J. Wilkes Booth. Was greatly shocked and distressed to hear it, because I do not think a shameful murder can advance any good cause, and I fear the mind of Europe will be easily persuaded that Booth was prompted to commit the horrible crime by Confederates. I was especially pained to learn that he profaned the motto of Virginia *"Sic Semper Tyrannes,"* by shouting it from the stage just before making his escape. When I returned to the West End I found the whole mighty metropolis in a state of the most intense excitment at the news. I have never before witnessed such a sensation in London.[12]

The news of the war did not greatly alter the tenor of life in London. Thompson seemed almost relieved. The Confederacy had lost and Richmond was burned, but this and worse had been anticipated for months. At least his family, though impoverished, had survived, and the killing was over. Thompson, however, was now faced with finding new employment to increase support of his family. Fortunately, *The Index* continued on until June. On the eighteenth of that month, he made an engagement with Captain Humber of the *Standard:* "I am to have one leader a week for a guinea and a half a week."[13] It was enough to keep him going, but he was forced to write his sister that the money and boxes, which he had sent regularly while his employment lasted, would have to be curtailed.

He wrote articles for several of the major English publications, including *Blackwood's Magazine* and perhaps *Cornhill's Magazine,* besides those for the *Standard.* Early in June, however, he found work that, although temporary, was steady while it lasted, and it paid well. In February of that year, Heros Van Borcke, who had served as chief of staff to General J. E. B. Stuart, arrived in London with his notes on the war. Van Borcke wanted to publish these notes in the form of a book-length memoir, for the English were eager to read about the war. He doubted his own abilities as a writer, however, so he hired Thompson, with whom he was already acquainted, to ghost-write the book for him. On July 15, he noted in his diary, "fifty-six closely written pages of Van Borcke's

Journal" which he had written during the week were sent off to *Blackwood's*. On August 31, he received fourteen pounds as his share for Part One of the Memoirs, which were being published serially in *Blackwoods* over a ten-month period. Thompson received about seventy dollars a month for his work, but no recognition. When the book was published in October, 1866, as *Memoirs of the Confederate War for Independence* by Heros Van Borcke, Thompson's name was not mentioned.

On November 15, 1865, he called again on Thomas Carlyle.

Found the Irish patriot Gavan Duffy there. Carlyle gave us a graphic account of a visit to the thieves' quarter in Whitechapel. He also spoke of the great ignorance of the educated classes in England and Germany of German history and literature....

Jan. 11, 1866 — Twelve inches of snow fallen. Nothing can be more dismal than a fall of snow in London. No matter how densely fall the flakes, they are scarcely more numerous than the flakes of soot; there is no sparkling surface as there is on snow in America. Lunched with Dean and Lady Stanley at the deanery, Westminster. The dean took us into the famous Jerusalem chambers, attached to the abbey, — a room hung with Arras tapestry, and where, according to Shakespeare, Henry VII died on the floor. In the dean's dining-room was a collection of the portraits of former deans: one of them was the famous Atterbury.[14]

At the beginning of 1865, Thompson had enlarged the field of his contributions and had begun to write as the London correspondent for American publications. For the *Cosmopolitan* he wrote several leaders, and he wrote weekly letters to the Louisville *Journal*. He also had plans, at least, for writing for the *Crescent Monthly* of New Orleans on European matters, but this was not to start till May. In April, the *Crescent* announced the event:

John R. Thompson, formerly editor of the *Southern Literary Messenger,* and well-known Virginian poet, is in London, writing for *Blackwoods,* and other English periodicals. As soon as his present literary tasks are complete, Mr. Thompson will become our regular foreign contributor, and we do not hesitate to say that a more valuable man could not be found.[15]

The May issue, however, carried only the poem, "Lee to the Rear."

By this time he was also furnishing a weekly letter to the New

Orleans *Picayune.* He was also plotting once more to bring out an anthology of Southern poems to be published by Bennett, a London publisher. The plan for this volume was evidently to be very similar to the book which had been lost on its way to London. Once again his plans were doomed to failure, although we do not know why.

Thompson's attention was briefly diverted from writing when he received a request from the president of William and Mary college in Williamsburg, Virginia. The College had been badly damaged during the war and wished Thompson to serve as its representative in England and Ireland to solicit and collect contributions toward the restoration of the College. Thompson was appealed to as "a distinguished representative of Virginia literature and a worthy example of the character which this college has pre-eminently contributed to foster among Virginians."[16] He accepted the mission and as part of his duty called on the Archbishop of Canterbury.

March 5 — Had by invitation an interview with his Grace the Archbishop of Canterbury on the subject of rebuilding William and Mary College. It lasted twenty minutes. He listened respectfully to all I had to say. He was very cautious not to utter a word on the American War, and I was cautious not to base my appeal for the college on exclusive church grounds. When I rose to leave, he promised his favor and assistance. In the evening went to see Tennyson, at Lady Franklin's, Kensington Gore. The bard was ill with a cold but received me genially. . . . [17]

His efforts on behalf of William and Mary were not highly successful. He collected some money, however, including a contribution from the Archbishop, and was moderately successful in soliciting books from the publishing houses of London and Edinburgh. For these efforts he was awarded an honorary Master of Arts degree in 1866.

London still had great interest in Thompson or people with interesting stories to tell; he wrote in his diary, for example:

March 19 — Dined at Mr. Schenley's Prince's Gate. He showed me a beautiful emerald ring given him by Lord Byron, engraved with devices in Arabic, the signet-ring of some pasha. Referring to Byron, he said he knew him well in Italy, — that he was a coarse lubberly man and that all who knew him marvelled at his success with women, which could not be imputed to his good looks. Shelley he describes as having a feminine appearance and great gentleness of manner. Mr. Schenley was present with Trelawney and assisted at the burning of Shelley's remains. He said that the Countess of Guiccioli was never pretty, even in her *premiere jeunesse.*[18]

But even London was not enough to keep Thompson's mind from wandering back to Virginia, and he began to think seriously about returning. He had never been content or really willing to leave his father and sister in Richmond, and his fears for their safety and well-being caused him many sleepless nights in London. Undoubtedly, his usefulness to the family had been greater in London, where he could buy things at reasonable prices to send back to Richmond; and now his usefulness was still greater. Making enough to send boxes regularly again, he had sent money to his father to restock his store, burned in the evacuation. On several occasions father and sister had urged him to "stay where you are at present." This was as much out of consideration for his own health as it was for them. Health standards were very low in Richmond, nor was there work to be had. Yet he wrote in his diary of his longing for home:

April 7 — I envy everyone going home. I long to see dear old Virginia. I love her deeper for her impoverishment. Her wasted fields seem more beautiful than this richly-cultured England. As for the best class of people there, I am convinced, as I compare them with the aristocracy of other countries, they are higher in the scale of moral elevation than any [other?] class on earth, and so thinking, I ask, "Am I worthy to be a Virginian?"[19]

Now that the war was over, another set of Americans were coming to England, not to escape war nor campaign for English support, but to enjoy a holiday after the weary years. Mrs. Robert C. Stanard, who had been his patron and support in those early years with the *Messenger,* came to England with her son Hugh, one of Thompson's closest friends from childhood, and he was sorely tempted to return with them.

By this time Thompson had a very solid core of good friends with whom he spent many evenings at dinner, games of whist — he was a much-sought-after partner — the theater and parties. Chief among these was Anne Thackeray and her younger sister. She remembered him later in a letter to his friend William Gordon McCabe:

His was the first new face that came into our house when we began life again after my dearest Father's death, and I remember the strange first feeling, and then somehow he seemed at once to have belonged to our old home and old days so naturally did we make friends.[20]

He spent a great deal of time with Anne, who made it a point to see that he was invited to her own functions and to those which she attended. Sometime before he left England she gave him, out of her father's love for him, the copy of *Henry Esmond* which the author had inscribed for his family, "For my dearest mother and Children, W. M. T. Oct. 27, 1852."[21]

Also a great friend by this time was Carlyle in whose home Thompson spent several evenings every month. Alfred Lord Tennyson was another whose home and friendship had been opened to him. Tennyson had first met Thompson at the home of the sculptor and poet Thomas Woolner, a member of the preRaphaelite group. A year later they met again in Woolner's home, when Tennyson was more animated and "proved a pleasant conversationalist when he entertained the party with talk on nightmares and murder."[22] Tennyson, recalling the same evening, wrote, "Thompson the Confederate was there and Browning, and innumerable anecdotes were told."[23] Later that year Thompson visited Tennyson.

June 30, 1866 — went with Bertrand Payne, Esq. to Lymington, thence by ferry to Yarmouth, where we took a carriage to Ferringford, the residence of Tennyson, and were warmly received by him. A lovelier spot would be difficult to find. An irregular Gothic cottage, surrounded by beautiful trees, the ilex and the elm, and exquisite turf, and with glimpses of the sea from almost every window, abundant roses, and a thrifty magnolia grandiflora growing on the south wall, nailed up like apricots, and almost secluded from the world. All was charming; books everywhere, engravings, a few paintings, casts, and statuettes. Dined at seven. Mrs. Tennyson, a most gentle lady in evident feeble health, with remains of rare beauty, the poet's sister, an old maid, his boys Hallam and Lionel, this was the family. After dinner, which was excellent but simple, — soup, salmon, roast mutton, ducks, peas, tarts, puddings, strawberries, and cherries, — the gentlemen adjourned to the top of the house, where, in the poet's sanctum, we had pipes and talk till two o'clock.[24]

Another friend who came home to England with the end of the war was the brilliant young journalist of the London *Times,* Francis Lawley. He had left Richmond on the day the Federal troops entered; but before that he had written to his mother in England of his friendship with Thompson and asked her to entertain him. In September of 1865 the two friends travelled up to York. On the way back Thompson visited the Lake Country and viewed the memorial window in the church at Ambleside. Thompson had been one of the American contributors to the installation of this window in memory of Wordsworth.

Eventually, not even the exalted company of Anne Thackeray, Tennyson, Carlyle, Lawley, Woolner, Owen, and Palgrave, or the less intimate friends such as Browning, Tyndale, Mallais, Lord Houghton, Holman Hunt, Hope, Latrobe, Landseer, Dickens — whom Thompson had come to admire after at first thinking him vulgar — and Wilkie Collins, could keep him in England. Against all the advice of his friends and family, Thompson decided to give up a promising and rapidly expanding literary life in London to return to Richmond:

Sept. 6 — took my final leave of London, after a residence of more than two years. . . .
Sept. 11 — Left Birmingham with satisfaction, a bustling, crowded, vulgar, dirty town. Rain, rain everywhere. Went by rail *via* Chester to Bangor.
Sept. 15 — Sailed in the steamer *Cuba* for New York.[25]

The Southern Literary Messenger perished in June, 1864. The *Examiner* also had ceased publication, and John M. Daniel was dead. The ranks of friends whom Thompson knew in and around Richmond were dead or dispersed, for the most part. There were now fewer publications than before the war, and these lacked the wartime popularity of Richmond periodicals. Richmond was no longer the capital of a rebel nation, and there were no jobs to be had. All of this Thompson knew before he gave up his budding career in London. Why did he do it? Why not, if he wanted to see Richmond and his family, make a short trip back and then return to London? A return to London — though in many ways his London years were the happiest of his life — seems never to have occurred to Thompson. The work he was doing for the *Standard* could have been interrupted and then resumed. His correspondence for American periodicals could have been continued, even expanded, after a trip to America. He might even have published the book of Southern poetry on which he had been working in London, had he returned. Instead, with singleminded determination, he set his sights on America and Virginia, and, as far as we know, he never looked back.

After a rough trip from Liverpool, in September of 1866 Thompson landed in Boston. He was so eager to see Richmond that he ignored his father's suggestion that he stop to visit relatives in Concord. He started south immediately, stopping only briefly in New York to visit the Lounsberys at his sister's request "for Ma's sake," and in Baltimore to visit his niece Mary Lewis. When he arrived in Richmond, he found the city more changed than he had imagined. War, fire, looting, and vandalism had destroyed much of the city, and business had almost stopped. The following January, he wrote B. Johnson Barbour of his reaction:

I dread another civil war, a fire dances before me and a sound of armed men rings now in my ears. The Radicals are bent upon destruction. It is the fury of the Jacobins over again. God preserve you, my dear friend, whom I hold a better man than Virgniaud, from the fate of the Geronde.[26]

What little work Richmond had to offer was manual labor, for the most part, not writing. His health would not allow him to take such jobs as were available, and there were no offers within the range of his capabilities. He appealed to all of the newspapers and periodicals of Richmond for employment, but not even his old friend and protege, George W. Bagby, who had succeded Thompson as editor of the *Messenger* and later as correspondent to the *Memphis Appeal* — both at Thompson's recommendation — could or would give him employment. He expressed his mortification and distress to Barbour in January, 1867:

You will say this is either unmanly despondence or ungrateful murmuring. Not so, my friend, you wholly misapprehend my feeling about Virginia. I was very far from thinking that I had been badly treated. I was one of the least worthy of Virginia's sons and have done nothing to do her credit or honor. But it *was* and *is* disheartening to know that in my native town I was not wanted and could not make my bread. While I was in Richmond, two or three places in journalism were filled which I should have been glad to secure, but although the proprietors of the papers (who were my friends) *knew this* fact, they did not think well enough of my talents to make me an offer for my services. But more than enough of this.[27]

Turning from a career in journalism, Thompson became briefly a lecturer. After Christmas of 1866, he went to Louisville, Kentucky, where he lectured before an appreciative audience. "But for the weather," he wrote Barbour, "I should have made a very handsome little pile, for the public expectation had been raised to a high point. The night, however, was the very worst of the winter and one of the worst I ever saw. It really was at risk of life and limb that one went out of the house...but I had an audience of 250." He remained in Louisville ten days and gave a second lecture. In New Orleans, his next stop, he spoke to large gatherings under the sponsorship of the Southern Hospital Association, whose trustees included Beauregard, Hood, and Longstreet. His regular presentations for these lectures included "English Journalism," "The Life and Genius of Edgar A. Poe," and "Fools." But even the lecture tour was almost an accident, for he had gone to Louisville to attend a wedding and was "entreated to linger beyond my time by an invitation from Guthrie, Prentice, Kirby Smith, and other prominent citizens to lecture here...."[28] This he wrote to Burton Harrison, and to him he wrote again on March 2 from Richmond:

While I should prefer living in New York to any place in this country, yet it would be little short of madness in me to encounter the risks of success and failure there as a literary man and a journalist, without a certain reliance in a connection with some established paper. Of all avocations, nothing is so precarious as literature....You do not know, my dear fellow, the heart sickness that waits upon constant failure. *I do.* I have failed all my life. I lingered in New York two weeks in October to try to get work. I didn't care what sort....But if I were ever so much disposed to come to New York and attempt writing, outside of a regular employment on an established journal, *I couldn't,* because I am utterly penniless and couldn't pay my way a fortnight....[29]

By April, he had changed his mind. He was still in Richmond and looking for steady employment, for the lecture tour was not reliable; and finding nothing promising, he decided to try the Bohemian life in New York:

Having satisfied myself beyond all question that there is no career for me here, no hope of employment even, I am just on the eve of departure for New York, where I shall remain *en permanence* if the fates are propitious. I have nothing certain before me, and only go to 'brest the blows of circumstances and grapple with my evil star'. The Bohemian life is dreary enough in the prospect of it, and my heart is sad almost to breaking in sundering the tie that binds me to Virginia, but I must get to work at something and the sooner the better.[30]

He reached New York in April of 1867. Before him was a year of loneliness, poverty, embarrassment, and longing for his home on Leigh Street, for the friends he had left, Mrs. Stannard, Bagby, McCabe and Cooke. He was connected with a number of journals for short periods of time, doing hackwork; later, with Thackeray's friend William Young, who was publishing *Every Afternoon,* a publication on the style of the *St. James Gazette.* Unfortunately, *Every Afternoon* lasted only four weeks. He also contributed to *The Land We Love;* to this Charlotte, North Carolina, publication he contributed almost every month from May 1867 to February 1868, excepting only October and December.

Still, Thompson could not have chosen a more promising city in which to find literary work. In the seven years from 1863 to 1870, New York had seen five journals of major importance established there, *The Round Table* (1863), *The Nation* (1865), *The Galaxy* (1866), *Appleton's* (1869), and *Scribner's Monthly* (1870). There were numerous lesser magazines which came and went, sometimes within a few weeks. By 1865, despite the failures, New York was doing far more publishing than her two traditional rivals, Boston and Philadelphia. In fact, New York became after the Civil War the undisputed leader among American cities as a mecca for writers from all over the country. It was also at this time that the dominant emphasis in American literature shifted from romance to realism, a shift which was virtually complete by 1875. The interest created in reporting during the Civil War was one of the noticeable influences in effecting this change. While Thompson did not himself change overnight and maintained something of his sentimentalism to the end of his days, he was much more aware of the changing tastes than were many of his friends, including, for example, Richard Henry Stoddard, Edmund C. Stedman, Bayard Taylor, Thomas Bailey Aldrich and Richard W. Gilder, a group whose dedication to the older genteel tradition was not shaken by the revolution in taste and thought all around them. Curiously, however, it was not the blindness of his Northern friends that Thompson noted, but that of his Southern colleagues. To one correspondent he wrote, "The trouble with Southern writers is that they will *not* turn from the old sorrows, the lost cause, the humiliation of the dear old land, to write about things that are current *here*....Good, terse, pointed literary work, be it magazine writing or newspaper paragraphs, is always sure of a purchaser in this city."[31] To George Bagby, whose book on John M. Daniel had been rejected by several

Northern publishers, he wrote:

Moreover he [Daniel] is the dead representative of a buried principle, the
dumb champion of a lost cause, the inefficient type of a race now extinct,
and all interest in him, his writings and his country has quite faded out.
My dear fellow, at Appomattox C[ourt] H[ouse] we lost not merely State
Sovereignty, free government, all that we had been fighting for during 47
years of trial, but the ear, the attention of mankind. Our fight became a
rebellion and a stigma was attached to all of us that were engaged in it.
The world's now indifferent to us, its pulses are languid at the recital of
our brave deeds, and it receives with apathy anything we may address to
it.[32]

Certainly these are bitter pronouncements, but they are expressed
with a style, vigor and wisdom which had not previously characterized Thompson's writings.

In all probability Thompson was for a while employed by
William Young in another of his enterprises, the translation of
Victor Hugo's *L'Homme Qui Rit.* Paul Hamilton Hayne, at least,
was of this impression, and that Thompson had done the majority
of the work, if not all of it. He asked Thompson, in late 1869, "Did
you translate V. Hugo's novel in *Appleton?* Miss Jeanne Dickerson
wrote me to that effect, & I suppose she was not mistaken. Indeed,
I hope not, because the translation is *wonderful* & ought to have
brought you a *small fortune.*"[33] It is more likely Thompson
collaborated with Young, but Thompson's answer to Hayne is not
now extant.

On February 1, 1868, Thompson published a poem, inspired
perhaps by the suffering of children he had seen in Europe, titled
"Misirrems, or A Local Item" in *Harper's Weekly,* with illustra-
tions. It tells the story of the death of a New York beggar boy —
somewhat in the style of George Crabbe, tragic realism in rhyming
couplets. It is filled with much trite diction and not a little of
almost-sarcasm — or, at least, misplaced levity. It was an unusual attempt for Thompson and may have been an expression
of his own suffering over the last ten years, certainly of the pain he
had seen around him in war and poverty. It is not successful as a
poem and had little to recommend it, but the last verse paragraph is
strong and good — as Longfellow is good, when he is.

Sometime in the spring of 1868, a friend asked Thompson to
write some book reviews. He was sufficiently impressed to show
them to William Cullen Bryant, editor of the New York *Evening*

Post. After a trial period in May, Thompson was offered the position of literary editor, a post which only Bryant himself had occupied since he first came to the *Post* in 1829. Thompson, however, had some slight misgivings about accepting a position on a newspaper which had for a long time expressed an unequivocally hostile attitude toward the South. He told Mr. Bryant that he was a Southerner and his convictions would not change, but that if Bryant still wished to hire him, he would be very glad to accept. He had also consulted his family and friends in Virginia, and all agreed that it would not be unloyal to work for the *Post.* Parke Godwin of the *Post* records that everyone from Bryant down respected Thompson for his devotion when he was so obviously in financial need. Bryant himself saw to it that no book was placed on Thompson's desk for review which could hurt his feelings.

The offer of the position of literary editor by Bryant was a rather remarkable occurrence. It came as something of a shock to those who knew the history of the *Post.* In all the thirty-nine years of Bryant's connection with the paper, no regular chair had been established. In 1860, William Dean Howells had unsuccessfully applied for such a position, and so had Park Benjamin sometime later. There seems nothing peculiar about Bryant's change of mind, however. He himself had done most of the work of the literary editor and enjoyed it. In 1868, however, he was immersed in his translation of *The Iliad.* He was almost seventy-four and evidently felt the need of editorial assistance. Certainly Thompson was as well qualified as any man then available. He came highly recommended by Thompson's and Bryant's mutual friends William Gilmore Simms and Edmund C. Stedman, and perhaps Richard Henry Stoddard as well. It was Stedman who had introduced Thompson to Bryant. Thompson was well read in European and American literature of his times. He had gained the polish and experience that so cosmopolitan a paper as the *Post* required, and he had a well-established reputation as a poet and critic. Finally, his gentle nature and cultivated social graces endeared him as a companion to Bryant.

Thompson seems to have been almost universally liked and respected by his fellow workers on the *Post.* One of his colleagues at that time, Watson R. Sperry, who would later be managing editor, wrote that Thompson was a "Rebel to be loved.... A lot of tall, straggling Virginia gentlemen, ex-soldiers, I fancy, all of them, began to visit the office. Mr. Thompson had a big man's beard, a

delicate body, and a sensitive feminine nature. He was a bit
punctilious, but kindness itself.''[34] The passage of time and the
decay of health and fortune were obvious also, but his powers of
conversation and mind were still impressive. Bryant thought him
the most charming conversationalist in New York society:

He had read so variously, observed so minutely, and retained so tena-
ciously the results of his reading and observation. . .that he was never at a
loss for a topic and never failed to invest what he was speaking of with a
rare and original interest. His fund of anecdote was almost inexhaustible,
and his ability to illustrate any subject by apt quotation no less
remarkable.[35]

Both John Esten Cooke and Richard Henry Stoddard also thought
him an unexcelled storyteller.

From the time of Thompson's association with the *Post,* the
newspaper's practiced antiSouthern attitude abated somewhat.
Also notices about Southern matters appeared frequently. For
example, William N. White, Thompson's friend from his *Southern
Field and Fireside* days, published a book on horticulture, and
Thompson reviewed it, characterizing his friend as a "skillful horti-
culturalist" and his book as authoritative. He also noted the visit of
President Ewell of William and Mary College to New York, and reviewed William Cabell Rives' *Life of James Madison,* praising his
fellow Virginian while still noting the faults of the book.[36] In
January, 1869, he wrote an announcement of the reorganization of
the Virginia Historical and Philosophical Society, with which he
and B. B. Minor and George W. Bagby had all been associated in
the past and which Thompson four months later was asked to join
as a "corresponding member."

Also, through personal contacts he helped many of his old
friends who came to New York in whatever ways he could. Of
course, not all of his dealings with his Southern friends were happy.
By 1872, some of his acquaintances had become nuisances. To
McCabe, he wrote in complaint:

Only think of a sensible man like _____ writing me as follows:
"My dear Thompson: I take the liberty of sending to you this morning a
manuscript entitled '_____' to ask if you can have it published in
Appleton's Journal, or any other periodical of equal value. I would have
sent it direct to Appleton had I been known to him, or 'had the manuscript
merit enough to speak for itself'''!!

Isn't this goring? What is a man to do when such a man as _____ expects him to have manuscripts published in a journal with which he has no sort of connection, irrespective of the manuscript's merits? And isn't it absolutely preposterous that I should be used by all the people in the South who wish to be contributors to Northern magazines as an eleemosynary agency for their literary undertakings?[37]

Generally, however, he was willing to do what he could, and he never expressed his disgust in any medium more public than the private letter.

As literary editor, he exerted great influence on the attitude of the *Post.* He had wide general powers to act and write as he pleased, but he was called on to do a variety of duties. He wrote reviews and literary material, acted as special correspondent on several occasions, such as when he attended the musical "Jubilee" in Boston in June 1872, and he reviewed plays and musical performances. His book review work consisted of "scissors work and tepid comment," in which he restricted his commentary to brief highlights of the subject between long quotations. But he also wrote criticisms as full and as good as any of those written for the *Southern Literary Messenger.*

The first of the two types of reviews was necessitated by the requirements of a daily newspaper. He selected representative passages which demonstrated the style or gave interesting parts of the book. In such fashion he reviewed Longfellow's *New England Tragedies,* Edmund C. Stedman's *The Blameless Prince,* and Emerson's *Society and Solitude.* For Froude's *History of England,* he quoted the two most interesting episodes — the execution of Mary Stuart and the defeat of the Spanish Armada — giving the reader the history at its best.

Allen Nevins in his history of the newspaper summed up Thompson's contribution to Bryant's paper, thus:

Unfortunately, Thompson added little to the *Post's* literary reputation. In large part this was because of his wretched health, for he steadily wasted away with consumption, was much out of the office, and maintained his energy only by following his doctor's orders to take large doses of whiskey. . . .

Even had his health been sound and his critical faculties the best, Thompson could not have made the *Post* a good literary organ in the present-day sense. It did not want critical or analytical reviews. An entertaining summary or paraphrase would appeal far more to the general reader. Moreover, there was a feeling that American literature was a delicate organism, which needed petting and might have its spirit broken by harsh words. Mr. Towse justly says of Thompson: "His condemnation was apt to be expressed in terms of modified praise. He confined himself largely to what was explanatory or descriptive, though his articles were written fluently and elegantly, were interesting, and had a news, if no great descriptive, value."[38]

The *Post* as a newspaper had no pretentions to literary quality, and its columns were singularly devoid of permanent literary interest. There were, however, occasional poems from minor, and usually, local poets; but Bryant wrote several poems for the paper also, and these are almost the only works of lasting interesting from this time. Thompson was successful, however, in that he gave the paper and its readers what they wanted.

The occasional sparks of critical insight that came during these last years are to be found in such reviews of his as the one on Hawthorne's *Passages from the American Notebooks.* Here he displays impressive critical powers in discussing Hawthorne as an author. Similarly, in his essay on Browning's *The Ring and the Book,* judging both story and author, he accurately predicts that "Pompilia" will prove most popular:

These are lines of great vigor, expressions that are original and striking, long passages which display a vivid imagination and admirably depict the moods, thought and passions of the speaker....Perhaps its highest value may ultimately be found not in the author's ambitious analytical studies of character, but in such an anthology of rich, forcible, pointed, witty and proverbial sayings.[39]

Of Mark Twain's *Innocents Abroad,* Thompson wrote in praise of the humor, "cleverness, frankness, and catholic spirit," but he thought that the book would have been "more creditable to the author's well established reputation had it been less by two-thirds."[40] Of equal quality were his reviews of John Forster's *Life of Walter Savage Landor,* in which he was able to use his considerable knowledge of England and Florence, and of Heinrich Heine's *The Last Thoughts of a Poet,* a posthumous collection of Heine material. "As a master of tender sentiment and exquisite simplicity in melodious verse," he wrote, "Goethe alone is his equal among the writers born to use the German tongue....His sturdy and consistent assertation of the intellectual freedom, his fiery enthusiasm in the great way of humanity against privilege, his fierce scorn of all shams and lies, deserves to be rendered into every tongue and transfused through every literature."[41] Thompson then went on to give his own translation of Heine's "Wo?" — "The Grave Song."

> Where shall yet the wanderer jaded
>   In the grave at last recline?
> In the South, by palm trees shaded?
>   Under lindens by the Rhine?
>
> Shall I in some desert sterile
>   Be entombed by foreign hands?
> Shall I sleep, beyond life's peril,
>   By some seacoast in the sands?
>
> Well! God's Heaven will shine as brightly
>   There as here, around my bed,
> And the stars for death-lamps nightly
>   Shall be hung above my head.[42]

Thompson also did an excellent job of reviewing W. M. Rossetti's *Edition of the Works of Shelley*. This was a labor of love and personal interest. He had perhaps never met any of the three famous Rossettis; but he did know several members of the preRaphaelite Brotherhood, including Thomas Woolner, Holman Hunt, John Everett Millais, so he had an indirect interest in Rossetti. Also, of course, Shelley had been one of his favorite poets from early youth. Of Shelley he wrote:

His actual achievements place him high among the poets of the whole world; and if we are required to judge of his capacity, we can only say that, had the career of every poet known to us ended with his thirtieth year, the foremost name of all the human race, the poet of poets would be Percy Bysshe Shelley.[43]

Surprisingly, when Dante Rossetti's poems were published in 1870, Thompson treated them with little interest. He praised the book as a whole, noted some minor faults, commented on the beauty of the volume, but little more.

A work that should have been a great challenge to Thompson was the review of Bryant's translation of *The Iliad*. Bryant selected Thompson to write the review, but there is little reason to think that

Bryant was testing him or that he expected an automatic approval from his employee. Still, Thompson, who must have felt some pressure, made a rather mechanical essay of the review. He demonstrated his familiarity with other translations and accurately judged the strengths of Bryant's work, but there was no great praise or criticism or illuminating insight. Bryant evidently was satisfied, for he asked Thompson to review the second part of the translation when it came from the presses.

Thompson also wrote some miscellaneous literary essays on subjects of current interest. Among these are "Russian Literature," "Pacific Coast Literature," "Mystery Plays," and "Literature in Great Britain during 1870." To these he added articles of popular interest. At Christmas time, for example, he informed his readers at which shops toys, new games, fancy goods, and gold and silver gifts were available. He wrote letters also on special occasions or when out of town. Bryant also sent letters to help Thompson fill out the columns.

On one of Bryant's holidays, in March of 1872, word reached him that Thompson's health was failing fast. He immediately invited Thompson to join him in Havana, Cuba. Bryant used the ruse of having Thompson come down to Cuba to help him write letters back to the *Post;* but after one letter, Thompson's doctors ordered him not to exert himself even that much. Thompson made a partial recovery and returned to New York. Later that year, he was writing more letters for the *Post* when he reported on the music Jubilee from Boston. Nevins, for one, considered these travel letters among the best work Thompson did for the *Post.*

In summing up Thompson's work as literary editor of the *Post,* it can be said that, as always, he was competent, judging accurately what was asked of him by his readers and his editor-in-chief. His reviews and essays, taken as a whole, were above average for a newspaper and often ranked with the best critical assessments of the times. His informal essays were always entertaining and well written, still showing the influence of Lamb. That Thompson was a "half-invalid" fettered by inadequate funds and a reading public little interested in literature as such, surely all stand in mitigation of the mediocre quality of the *Evening Post* between the years 1868-1873. Taken overall, however, Thompson's work compares favorably with that of the editors of *Scribner's, Lippencott's,* and *Appleton's.*

During this five-year period, Thompson wrote an occasional

sketch or poem for other periodicals, *Scribner's, Appleton's* and *Lippencott's* in particular. The *Post* printed a popular poem of this period, a translation of Gustaves Nadaud's "Carcassone" signed by M. E. W. Sherwood, which inspired Thompson to try the same poem. Watson R. Sperry remembered, "His most famous poem, the translation of Nadaud's 'Carcassone', was written in the *Evening Post* office — the unfinished manuscript was kicking around on his desk for several days,...but published in *Lippencott's;* its popularity rather irritated him."[44] Nevertheless, Thompson sent copies of it to a number of friends and seemed pleased enough with it then and with their compliments. Thompson's translation is more exact than that of Sherwood. The original final quatrain is

> Nous partines le lendemain,
>   Mais, que le Bon Dieu lui pardonne,
> Il mourut a moitie chemin,
>   Il n'a jamais vu Carcassone.

Sherwood had written:

> That night there came for passing soul the
>   Churchbell's low and solemn toll
> He never saw gay Carcassone
> Who has not known a Carcassone.

Thompson rendered the lines:

> We left next morning his abode,
>   But (heaven forgive him) half way on
> The old man died upon the road;
>   He never gazed on Carcassone —
> Each mortal has his Carcassone![45]

Both are somewhat guilty of liberties with the original and violate the poetic intention by stressing the overt moral; but Thompson's translation is more readable and follows the French, generally better. Most important, however, is the fact that Thompson's was quite popular and helped to popularize Nadaud's poetry in America.

These poems were written in an effort by Thompson to become a steady contributor to other New York journals, but he met with little success. Several sketches, "Jailbirds and Their Flights," "Something about Balloons," and a notice of Mrs. M. J. Preston's "Old Songs and New," appeared in *Scribner's* as did "New Ways in the Old Dominion" under the pseudonym of Major Hotchkiss. He had also placed "Southern Sketches," a series of illustrated articles, in *Appleton's* in July and August, 1870. In 1872 the same journal published "Richmond, Historic and Scenic."[46]

Thompson spent much of his time in New York, as he had elsewhere, among friends, dining, talking, playing whist and billiards. He had relatives in the city, and his job soon expanded his circle of friends, among whom Bryant himself was a mainstay. Shortly after he took the *Post* position Thompson became a regular part of the Bryant household. Bryant wrote of him later:

It has rarely been our lot to be associated with a person who combined more completely the best characteristics of the Christian gentleman and the scholar than John R. Thompson. Endowed with warm and quick sensibilities of a native of the South, a keen sense of personal honor, and a chivalrous devotion to his friends and his cause, whatever it might be, he was yet so amiable in his disposition and so courteous in his conduct, that he made no enemies and won hosts of friends. No one, indeed, ever approached him without being impressed alike by his gentility, his integrity and his modesty.[47]

Other homes were opened to him also; the Isaac Hendersons, in particular, made him feel at home, as did the Nordoff family, both connected with the *Post*. When his final illness prevented his working and friends sent him to Colorado to recuperate, it was to the Hendersons' house he returned. His friend, James Wood Davidson, wrote of Mrs. Henderson:

Had she been his mother she could not have been more attentive,...more lovingly attentive than she was; and was uninterruptedly from the moment of his arrival until the end...by a thousand nameless sweet offices that flow from women's hearts to those they love.[48]

He also had friends among the publishers and editors of the city papers and magazines. In a letter to his sister in 1870 he described one of his days in New York:

I went to the great Free Trade Banquet at Delmonico's on Tuesday evening. It was an elegant affair altogether. I got a seat at the table with

Mr. Lavener, the editor of the "Drawer" in *Harper's Magazine,* Rev. Samuel Ireneus Prime of the *Observer,* Maj. Bundy of the *Evening Mail* and one or two other pleasant companions, and enjoyed myself exceedingly.[49]

Among the members of his family, Thompson seems to have found Mary Dyckman and Abbie Henderson (a niece of his father) the most congenial. He seems almost to regain his youth in their company, as a letter to his friend McCabe suggests:

Miss Mary and I (after a lunch at the Grevoort, the other day of filet aux champignons, green peas, strawberrys and cream and a bottle of Chateau Marguaz...) spent two hours very delightfully in the Aspenwall and Johnson Galleries, and wished for you, and I propose to ask her company to the Opera one evening this week where Kellog is singing. We shall go, of course, as *capita mortua;* although as I have just received a new satin crush hat and some pearl-coloured gloves from England, and shall go myself as a voluptuous swell, nobody will suspect us of free tickets.[50]

Relatives introduced him to their friends, and it was through the Dyckmans that he met Dr. Noah H. Schenck and his family. He became a familiar visitor in this home also at times, and it was Dr. Schenck who became his religious advisor in his last days.

Older contacts were not completely broken, of course; Thompson still maintained a correspondence with his friends in England and America. On one occasion in 1871, after receiving a letter from Tennyson, he wrote McCabe in youthful joy, but touched with a note of yearning:

I had a letter a fortnight ago from Mr. Tennyson written from his home in the Isle of Wight and kindly proposing, as he expresses it, to give me 'board and bed', if I will make him a second visit. Let us go, you and yours truly, and see Alfred, and talk to him about Arthurian days — high talk of noble deeds — and smoke the fragrant weed, and loaf about the lawn at Farringford, eating the lotus, drinking Bass his ale: my pensive Gordon, how is this for high?[51]

In addition, at least up to 1870, Thompson was still writing William Gilmore Simms, John Esten Cooke, Paul Hamilton Hayne, and others from his Richmond days.

Trips to nearby scenes were still a source of interest and amusement throughout his New York stay. He also had the trips to Cuba and Boston and another to Newport in 1872. He managed at least

one visit a year to his home in Richmond or Gordonsville to be with
his sister and father, who was now in his eighties and dependent on
his son for upkeep as well as interest in life. These were always
occasions of celebration for young and old, and Thompson never
neglected to bring gifts for everyone, including the great-nieces and
-nephews. He usually came home for Christmas when he could get
away from the *Post.* These journeys home were all the more dear to
him since he knew he was soon to die. The relentless tuberculosis
was now fast killing him; even while he laughed and smiled with
friends, he was straightening out his affairs, preparing fair copies
of his literary works, and writing his will, all in the same systematic
and orderly fashion as he had lived most of his life.

Thompson knew the hopelessness of his case, and most of those
who saw him recognized it also. He did not talk about it though,
and his letters home and to his friends made little mention of it. It
was, therefore, something of a shock to those who met him. The
editor of the *New Orleans Picayune,* who saw him when he went to
Cuba in 1872, remarked upon his appearance, ". . . last Easter,
when in company with Mr. Bryant he visited our city, it was but too
painfully apparent that the shadow of the dial had already fallen on
him."[52]

By January of 1873, it became obvious that if something could
not be done immediately, he could not survive. His physicians prescribed a trip to a more healthful environment than New York, and
despite the advice of friends Colorado was decided upon. Mr. Isaac
Henderson offered to pay for the trip. Thompson wrote his family
of his plans, and Mrs. Quarles answered:

I can only repeat what I said before, that I think *this* is the best place for
you at present. . . . You could come here, rest awhile & ascertain whether
the change is decided enough to be beneficial & if not, could then go to
Aiken, which though not perhaps an agreeable place, may be decidedly
preferred to Colorado in point of comfort. . . . Hope I shall hear your decision very soon — don't delay your departure, but leave at once & *please*
make up your mind to come here.[53]

The elder Thompson also added a note urging his son to come to
Virginia. Thompson might have been wiser if he had taken their
advice. His pulmonary disease had so far advanced that, probably,
no change of scene or climate could have saved him; but, at least,
he would have had to travel less. He would have been in a more

comfortable temperature, and been among friends. Yet, his doctors had ordered him to Colorado, so there he went.

Mrs. Quarles wrote him that she was reconciled to his decision, and friends made arrangements. He left New York in the middle of February, and for a while in March the change in scene effected a partial recovery. Then he was worse. The climate and location seemed more an irritant than a cure. To McCabe he complained in detail:

I wish I could tell you how much I enjoyed your letter of the 22nd March, or that I could encourage you to write to me again in the same delightful way by telling you something of this far-away outpost of civilization. But I can do neither. The Dr. has absolutely forbidden me the use of pen and ink, and his prohibition unfortunately finds its general enforcement in my own weakness. I cannot walk a hundred yards without prostration. I cannot go upstairs, and for want of an elevator have never yet been as high as the second story of this hotel. An incessant cough and gasping for breath break me down day and night, for I cannot sleep. This is a sad recital, for my time is fast running out in which to find restoration, and my money is also getting low under expenses greater than one meets in any capital in Europe. It is provoking enough that this stupid territorial town, with its bad cuisine, its wild mob of people, its dreadful manners and its utter lack of anything to interest one in its daily routine, takes more money from my pocket daily than would pay my expenses in Mayfair or on the Mediterranean. True, yonder are the Rocky Mountains, and in the streets of Denver you see the Noble Savage, the primitive Aborigine, in a lazy, dirty, degraded Yute or Ute, from his Reservation across the mountain, trading off a buffalo-robe for whiskey. How it irks me to pay this money when I think what comforts it would gain for me elsewhere! Better fifty years of Europe than a cycle in Cathay.[54]

Then the Colorado weather took a turn for the worse. Snow storms and freezing temperatures came with the beginning of April. To Mrs. Henderson he wrote on April 17:

My dear friend, I have been losing ground steadily beyond a doubt.... The doctors order me to leave Colorado. I shall go tonight in the train to Kansas City.... I am in doubt whether to go first to New York or Virginia but shall come directly to 54th Street [the Hendersons'], trust you will make me a bed somewhere downstairs, for I can not go up a single flight. I am wasted to a skeleton and am hardly able to dress myself.[55]

He arrived in Kansas City so weak that he wired for someone from the *Post* to meet him there. James Wood Davidson, his replacement on the *Post,* went to meet him, arriving on April 26; they started back that afternoon.

Mr. Henderson met them at the train station when they arrived in New York on the 29th and took Thompson to his home. Realizing that the end was near, Thompson sent for his family the same day. On Wednesday Thompson asked Richard Henry Stoddard to act as his literary executor.

At some time during those last years, he had been showing his collection of autographs and books to McCabe. He told McCabe of Thackeray's pronouncement in Richmond — that he was willing to be judged as a writer on *Henry Esmond* — and he showed McCabe the autographed copy of the novel given him by Anne Thackeray. McCabe, who admired Thackeray above all other authors, said he would rather have the *Henry Esmond* than any of the rest. Thompson promised he should have it when he died. Although McCabe forgot the incident, Thompson did not. He dictated to Mrs. Henderson his last letter:

Among my books there is a copy of "Henry Esmond" (three volumes) which I hereby give to W. Gordon McCabe, Petersburg, Va., with a request that he will write to Miss Anne Thackeray a long account of my last illness and give her my love.[56]

He was given holy communion around noon and was visited by friends, including Dr. Schenck, the Hendersons, Davidson, and Mr. Coffin. Around four o'clock he became unconscious. At exactly twenty-five minutes past five on Wednesday, April 30, Mr. Coffin closed his eyes.

His family arrived the next day, and services were held in the Henderson home on Friday. Among those gathered were Bryant, Parke Godwin, Davidson, Stoddard, Thomas Le Clear, W. F. Williams, Richard W. Gilder, Augustus Maverick and General Roger A. Pryor. Thompson's body was taken back to Richmond. On May 2, a meeting of citizens, the bar, the press, the alumni of the University of Virginia, and firends met in the hall of the House of Delegates and heard resolutions from Dr. George W. Bagby, James Pleasants, James McDonald, Thomas H. Wynne, and P. T. Moore. They appointed a committee, led by Governor Walker and other prominent citizens, to meet the funeral party at the Byrd Street station and escort it to St. Paul's Church, where Thompson had worshiped. Dr. Peterkin of St. James Church officiated. Thompson was buried in Hollywood Cemetary, where also rest James Madison, John Tyler, and Jefferson Davis, as well as his friend J. E. B. Stuart. On a shaft of Virginia granite were engraved the words, "The graceful poet, the brilliant writer, the steadfast friend, the loyal Virginian."

The day after Thompson's death, William Cullen Bryant paid the respects of one poet-journalist to another in the pages of the New York *Evening Post,* the foremost American journal of its day:

. . .Not unaware of the certainty of his fate he yet seldom gave way to despondency or lost his interest in the great movements of life. It was because his character and tastes had rendered life agreeable to him in so many ways (despite the dark clouds that war and disease had gathered over it) that he desired to live; and no less because he had properly estimated its ends and issues that he did not fear to die. He went away reluctantly, for he left behind him some that were dependent upon him and many that loved him well; but he went away peacefully, knowing where he had placed his trust for the future, and that the passage which we who gaze upon it from this side call Death is to those who gaze upon it from the other side the Dawn of a longer and nobler activity.[57]

In one respect, Thompson did not place his trust for the future in reliable hands. His literary executor, Richard Henry Stoddard, made some attempt, he says, to publish the manuscript work left in his care by Thompson. Failing to do so, he later made no further efforts. He sold Thompson's library at auction and turned over the money to the elder Thompson. Years later he sent two parts of the London Diary to Mrs. Quarles.[58] Much of the remainder of the autographs and manuscripts have been lost. In 1920 John S. Patton published the poems of Thompson, collected from journals and letters. The essay on *The Genius and Character of E. A. Poe* was discovered in 1929 and privately published in Richmond. Of course, the great bulk of Thompson's literary output is to be found in the pages of *The Southern Literary Messenger, The Southern Field and Fireside, The Southern Illustrated News, The Memphis Daily Appeal, The London Index,* and the *New York Evening Post,* and in numerous other periodicals to which he contributed.

John Reuben Thompson was essentially conservative and classical. His value to literature is difficult to estimate. For thirteen years he edited the most popular and influential literary journal in the South, and his value to those who sought his help is worthy of

note. He was instrumental in creating a love of literature throughout his nation and of encouraging a respect for the highest modes
of conduct; in doing so he helped pave the way for the great
comics, satirists and realists who were to follow in the latter part of
the nineteenth century. More particularly he insisted that the South
should have its own literary voice — and that a great awakening in
literature was sure to come. Such a surety kept alive a hope which
found its realization in the twentieth century. Finally, though
students of Poe have previously chosen to ignore Thompson's
testimony, he was and remains a valuable witness of the character
of the greater poet; as the singular spokesman of a unique time and
place in history, his articles and sketches also reflect a writer of importance, perhaps the most polished prose stylist of his age.

Notes and References

Chapter One

1. Charles Marshall Graves, "Thompson the Confederate," *The Lamp,* 26, No. 3 (October, 1904), 181.
2. Letter of John Esten Cooke, May 24, 1860. John R. Thompson Collection, University of Virginia Library (Hereafter, University of Virginia Library).
3. Letter of Miss Lily Quarles to John S. Patton. University of Virginia Library.
4. Letter of Mrs. H. W. Quarles to J. R. Thompson, August 3, 1866. University of Virginia Library.
5. B. Johnson Barber, from a photocopy of a Richmond newspaper, n.d. in University of Virginia Library.
6. "New Works," *Southern Literary Messenger,* 19 (October, 1849). 640. (Hereafter cited as *SLM)*
7. John R. Thompson, *Poems of John R. Thompson,* ed. John S. Patton (New York, 1920), p. 235.
8. Joseph Roddey Miller, "John R. Thompson: His Place in Southern Life and Literature," Unpublished Doctoral Dissertation, University of Virginia, 1930, p. 9.
9. Minutes of Faculty Meetings, University of Virginia, 1841-1842.
10. Thompson, *Poems,* p. 228.
11. *SLM,* 15 (March, 1849), 192.
12. MS, University of Virginia Library.
13. *SLM,* 14 (September, 1948), 556.
14. "Richmond before the War," *The Index,* May 11, 1865.
15. John Esten Cooke, "John R. Thompson," *Hearth and Home,* December 20, 1873.
16. A. C. Gordon, *Memories and Memorials of William G. McCabe* (Richmond 1925), I, 16.
17. J. E. Cooke, *Hearth and Home.*
18. Graves, p. 182.
19. M. V. Terhune, *Marion Harland's Autobiography* (New York, 1910) p. 243.
20. Letter of J. R. Thompson to B. B. Minor, September 15, 1847. University of Virginia Library.

21. Miller, p. 33.

22. Letter of J. R. Thompson to Thomas C. Reynolds, March 12, 1849. University of Virginia Library.

23. *SLM,* 13 (October, 1847), 641.

24. *SLM,* 30 (June, 1860), 467.

25. David K. Jackson, "Some Unpublished Letters of John R. Thompson and Augustin Louis Taveau," *William and Mary Quarterly,* 16 (April, 1936), 213-14.

26. *Ibid.,* p. 214.

27. *SLM,* 13 (November, 1847), 644.

28. John S. Patton, "Biography," in *Poems of John R. Thompson* (New York, 1920), p. xxi.

29. *Ibid.*

30. *SLM,* 14 (January, 1848), 57.

31. Miller, *in passim,* pp. 108-11.

32. Letter of J. M. Legaré to Thompson, November 13, 1849. University of Virginia Library.

33. Letter of J. R. Thompson to P. P. Cooke, October 17, 1848. University of Virginia Library.

34. Letter of J. R. Thompson to T. C. Reynolds, March 22, 1849. University of Virginia Library.

35. John O. Beaty, *John Esten Cooke, Virginian* (New York, 1922), p. 22.

36. Letter of John Tyler to J. R. Thompson, n.d. University of Virginia Library.

37. *SLM,* 13 (October, 1847), 584.

38. William P. Trent, *William Gilmore Simms* (New York, 1968), p. 104.

Chapter Two

1. John Esten Cooke, *Poe as a Literary Critic,* ed. N. Bryllion Fagan (Baltimore, Maryland, 1946), p. vii.

2. Mary E. Phillips, *Edgar Allan Poe: The Man* (Chicago, 1926), II, 1298-99.

3. Letter from J. R. Thompson to Philip Pendelton Cooke quoted in Arthur Hobson Quinn, *Edgar Allan Poe: A Critical Biography* (New York, 1941), p. 568. Here follows the paragraph on Poe.

Poe is not in Richmond. He remained here about 3 weeks, horribly drunk and discoursing "Eureka" every night to the audiences of the Bar Rooms. His friends tried to get him sober and set him to work but to no effect and were compelled at last to reship him to New York. I was very anxious for him to write something for me, while he remained here, but his lucid intervals were so brief and infrequent that it was quite impossible. "The Rationale of Verse" I took, more as an act of charity than anything else, for though exhibiting great acquaintance with the subject, it is altogether too *bizarre,* and too technical for the general reader. Poe is a singular fellow indeed.

Quinn's quotation is the same as John H. Whitty's in the Memoir of his *Complete Poems of Edgar A. Poe* (New York, 1918), pp. lxvi-lxvii, except that Quinn adds, properly, the "every night" in the second line and "indeed," in the last line.

4. Phillips. p. 1299.

5. *Ibid.,* p. 1303.

6. Quinn, p. 625.

7. As for the charge that Thompson's statement about being much in touch with Poe from the time the two met in 1848 until the poet's death, being overstated, the two summers in Richmond have already been noted. Between these two periods there is evidence that Poe wrote to Thompson at least six times between December 1848 and June 1849. Letters from Poe on December 7 and January 18 have been noted. In a letter to Fred W. Thomas dated February 14, Poe referred to a letter to Thompson "a day or two ago." More "Marginalia" with notes was sent on May 10, and on June 9, he wrote Thompson asking for ten dollars. To Annie Richmond on June 16 he referred to another request he had sent to Thompson, asking him not to hold the money sent by E. H. N. Patterson but to send it on to Poe in New York, which Thompson did. Thompson doubtless, responded to these letters — and there may have been more. Still, twelve letters exchanged in six months are reasonable justification for saying "We were in constant correspondence." See John Ward Ostram, *The Letters of Edgar Allan Poe* (New York, 1966), pp. 427, 444, 447, 451.

8. Quoted in Killis Cambell, *The Mind of Poe and Other Studies* (Cambridge, Mass., 1933), pp. 63-99. In this essay, Griswold charges Poe with being unamiable, arrogant, irascible, envious, cynical and misanthropic, totally lacking in moral susceptibility and sense of honor. And "He had a morbid excess, that desire to rise which is vulgarly called ambition, but no wish for the esteem or the love of his species; only the hard wish to exceed...that he might have the right to despise a world which galled his self-conceit."

9. From a typescript letter, University of Virginia Library.

10. Phillips, II, 1537.

11. *The Complete Works of Edgar Allen Poe,* ed. J. A. Harrison (New York, 1965), XVII, 403-05.

12. *SLM,* 15 (November, 1849), 694-97.

13. *SLM,* 16 (March, 1850), 172-87. J. E. Cooke, who edited this issue of the *Messenger* did not approve of Poe's style of criticism and wrote of him, some two or three years later in his essay, *Poe as a Literary Critic,* as "the author of...some of the fiercest, most savage, and most unfair criticism ever published in America...It is impossible to read the series of

criticisms collected in his works under the title *The Literati,* and fail to see that invective is the author's favorite style. . . . Nothing pleased this man of genius, busying himself with small things, more than minute criticism and dissection of the style of some eminent writer." pp. 1-2, 6, 13. John M. Daniel wrote the review for Cooke. Cutler Andrews wrote of him:

Daniel was a misanthrope, a cynic, and a somewhat unstable individual, who was easily provoked into controversy. He both despised men and used them, taking advantage of their meannesses and weak points and evaluating their intellectual caliber with marvelous exactness. From early youth he had shunned society, preferring instead a small circle of intimate friends. In later life he was a recluse who lived among his books and had a horror of visitors. To judge from his editorials, Daniel admired only two public men of his day, John C. Calhoun and Stonewall Jackson. He esteemed Calhoun for his depth and precision of thought, strength of character, and steady nerve; Jackson for the quickness of his perception, which the editor likened to that of Napoleon.

The South Reports the Civil War (Princeton, N. J., 1970), p. 31. Daniel's review of the Griswold edition recognized Poe as the genius of the age in literature, but Daniel felt that Poe would be remembered for only a few good pieces. He mentions most of the character faults noted by Griswold then makes an allusion to some even darker crime against the second Mrs. Allan, but says ". . . if true it throws a dark shade upon the quarrel and very ugly light upon Poe's character. We shall not insert it. . . ." p. 176.

In the March 1850 issue of the *Messenger,* Thompson in an editor's note wrote of Griswold as one who ". . . has done more, perhaps, than any other person living to incite the ambition of young authors, and to raise up a literary class among a people devoted almost exclusively to the pursuits of trade and the learning of the price-current. Of Mr. Willis it is scarcely necessary to say a word. He is at once an honorable gentleman and a brilliant writer. . . . The Editor regrets the tone of his contributor's remarks with regard to these gentlemen the more, because he happens to know (what doubtless his valued contributor did *not,)* that Mr. Poe had received frequent attentions at their hands which he was ever warmly to acknowledge. . . as for Mr. Lowell the article contains not one word too harsh for *him.*" XVI, 192.

14. Rufus W. Griswold, *Passages from the Correspondence and Other Papers of Rufus W. Griswold* (Cambridge, Mass., 1898), p. 263.

15. *SLM,* 16 (October, 1850), 634.

16. Charles Marshall Graves, "Thompson the Confederate," *The Lamp,* 29 (October, 1904), 181. Also Patton, *Poems of John R. Thompson,* p. xxxix.

17. Hervey Allen, *Israfel: The Life and Times of Edgar Allan Poe* (London, 1927), II, 766.

18. Letter to E. H. N. Patterson, quoted in Harrison, XVII, 403-05.

19. Miller, p. 87. Also Griswold, letter, p. 297.

20. In his letter to Griswold, April 2, 1850, Thompson wrote in closing, "I felt this [treatment of Poe] so keenly that I sent to Willis for the Home Journal an article, by an intimate friend of mine, tending to remove some of the nettles cast by my contributor on the poet's grave." Willis printed the article, noting that Thompson was in New York during the period pre- ceeding the March 1850 *Messenger* — Miller says he was in Washington — but the article, attributed to "A Southern Gentleman," is not by Thompson. References in the article indicate that it was probably written by Robert C. Stanard. The article contends that "Eureka" was not so phil- osophical as Daniels had made it out to be, that the poet should not be smeared in public, and that he had some noble qualities, but it then goes on to say, "I do not deny that there were shadows. The wayward disposi- tion and the checkered life, which are too often the heritage of genius, did indeed fall the lot of this gifted man." *Home Journal,* March 30, 1850.

21. Miller, p. 94.

22. Letter from J. R. Thompson to R. W. Griswold, December 21, 1849, University of Virginia Library. The opening paragraph reads: "I have too long delayed sending you the promised items of poor Poe, and I fear that what I now enclose will be of little value, scarcely sufficient to warrent their incorporation into the Life. Two letters of Cooke's and a short statement relative to his connection with the Allans, are all that I have been able to get together."

23. Thompson to Patterson, November 9, 1848, *The American,* April 11, 1889.

24. Allen, II, 766. Quinn refers to Poe's letters to Thompson, but he does not say how many there were between the summers of 1848 and 1849, pp. 612-13.

25. *Ibid.*

26. Edward C. Wagenknecht, *Edgar Allan Poe: The Man behind the Mask* (New York, 1963), p. 32. See also John C. Miller, *Building Poe Biography* (Baton Rouge, 1977), p. 73. Miller quotes a letter from George Hand Brown who speaks for Thompson's honesty, but Miller without ex- planation says Thompson did not prove a reliable witness.

27. Phillips, II, 1302.

28. Quinn, pp. 656-57. Probably for the last time in his life Thompson had an occasion to practice law when early in November of 1849, Rosalie Poe called on him to act as her attorney in an attempt to gain the copy- rights and proceeds from the sale of the new edition of Poe's works. Quinn writes, "Thompson politely but firmly demanded for her as 'the sister and *sole heir* of the deceased'," the copyrights and concluded, "I have written to Mr. Neilson Poe, as Miss Poe's attorney, directing the trunk of the de- ceased to be forwarded to me. If it should come, I will be careful to secure for you [Griswold] the lectures and whatever literary contents may be found in it." Thompson had found that Poe had left his trunk at the Swan Tavern in Richmond and ordered it to be sent to Neilson Poe in Baltimore,

but it was returned to Richmond, for it was among Rosalie's possessions when she died. On November 11, 1849, Thompson wrote again to Griswold, "The mail to-night brings me your letter of the 7th, together with a letter from Mr. S. D. Lewis, Mrs. Clemm's solicitor, on the subject of the Poe publication. Of course, the sale of the copyright of 'Tales and Poems' by the author himself to Wiley and Putnam puts an end to the claim of Miss Rosalie. . . .

"With regard to 'Annabel Lee' I did not by any means attribute your publication of it to inconsideration or improper motives. The fact is simply this — Poe sold it to both of us, and for high price too, and neither of us obtained anything by the transaction. I lost nearly as much by his death as yourself, as I paid him for a prose article *to be written,* and he owed me something at that time. . . . By the way, I have a lien on a copy of his 'Tales and Poems' which contained full marginal notes and corrections in his own hand writing. He was to give it to me, after a new edition had been published. If it has come into your hands, you will oblige me by sending it to me, after your labors are concluded." Quinn, pp. 656-57.

29. Thompson, *The Genius and Character of Edgar Allan Poe* (Richmond, 1929), p. 4.

30. *Ibid.,* p. 2. In this essay Thompson seems to think that he may have misjudged Poe's conduct for he quotes Poe as saying "The editor of the *Weekly-Universe* speaks kindly, and I find no fault with his representing my habbits as 'shockingly irregular'. . . [he] has fallen into a very natural error." In explanation of this statement, Thompson quoted, in a footnote, a letter of 1848 from Poe to George W. Evelath in which Poe wrote ". . . at these times only [in states of wild excitement] I have been in the practice of going among my friends; who seldom, or in fact never, having seen me unless excited, take it for granted I am always so. . . . In the meantime I shall turn the general error to account." In effect, Thompson seems to be saying that Poe may not always have been drunk when he seemed so, and Poe himself intentionally created the impression that he was drunk at times when he was not. This practice would have been in keeping with the unusual inaccuracies in the recounting of the events of his life which Poe gave to Griswold.

31. *Ibid.,* pp. 11-13.

32. *Ibid.,* p. 17.

33. *Ibid.,* p. 30.

34. *Ibid.,* pp. 39, 41. It is possible that William Gilmore Simms heard this lecture and had it in mind when he wrote Thompson in 1867, "[J. S.] Redfield, by the way, was enquiring after you very earnestly. He desires to engage your pen in a new biography of Poe, with which he desires to publish a new edition of Edgar. That you are the very person to do such a work better than anybody else, I have no question. Still the task, in his case, is a very difficult one, since all biography should be written *con*

amore, and the poor fellow was perpetually upsetting his own buckets of milk, to the disgust of friends and admirers. Still, you could do it, without violating the truth, and yet with some softening of its harsher aspects." *The Simms Letters,* V, 31.

Chapter Three

1. *SLM,* 14 (January, 1848), 59. Cited in Miller, p. 160, and in Graves, p. 186.

2. In the Editor's Table for February, 1850, pp. 125-27, Thompson wrote of P. P. Cooke, "The Poems which Mr. Cooke left behind are not the effusions of a mere versifier. — This poetic sensibility joined to love of the old romances, wrought out the 'Froissart Ballads'. . . . No one can read the 'Froissart Ballads' without the conviction that had the life of the author been spared he would not have failed to produce some imperishable work of genius. . . . Mr. Poe expressed himself to us in highest terms of the first three parts of the remarkable production ('The Chevalier Merlin')."

3. *SLM,* 24 (January, 1857), 80.

4. Jay B. Hubbell, *The Last Years of Henry Timrod, 1864-1867* (Durham, N. C., 1941), p. 70.

5. *SLM,* 13 (November, 1847), 645.

6. *SLM,* 14 (November, 1848), 700.

7. *SLM,* 13 (November, 1847), 645.

8. *Ibid.*

9. William R. Manierre, "A Southern Response to Mrs. Stowe," *The Virginia Magazine,* 69 (1961), 85-86.

10. *Ibid.,* pp. 86-87.

11. *SLM,* 18 (October, 1852). Thompson had extra copies of this review printed, and sent one to President Millard Fillmore. Also, Manierre, p. 88.

12. Thompson evidently wrote this essay because he could not get anyone else to do it for him. He wrote to J. E. Cooke on September 12, 1852, "Despairing of being able to get a good peppery review of "UTC" from another hand, I sat down yesterday to devote my own powers to satirical analysis to Mrs. Stowe, when after several hours' labour upon the article the mail brought me a letter from Holmes. . . . I have not, however, abandoned my own effort." Again, on September 23, he wrote to Cooke, "I have been hard at work on a review of 'Uncle Tom's Cabin' which I hope to finish tomorrow or the next day. It is to be slashing." University of Virginia Library. This was rather close to the deadline for the October issue. Thompson had still hoped to have Holmes's review up to the last minute.

13. Manierre, p. 88.

14. *Ibid.,* p. 90.

15. *SLM,* 18 (October, 1852), 630-38. Thompson began this essay as a literary review; he even grants Mrs. Stowe "a happy faculty of descrip-

tion, an easy and natural style, an uncommon command of pathos and considerable dramatic skill. . . ." He then proceeds to an *argumentum ad hominem* and concludes the review with a political comment. Mrs. Stowe, he states, "is only entitled to criticism at all, as the mouthpiece of a large and dangerous faction which if we do not put down with the pen, we may be compelled one day (God grant that day may never come!) to repel with the bayonet." Holmes appeared in *Messenger,* 18 (December, 1852), 721-31.

16. *SLM,* 19 (June, 1854), 321-30.

17. *Ibid.*

18. *SLM,* 18 (January, 1853), 61.

19. David K. Jackson, "Some Unpublished Letters of John R. Thompson and Augustin Louis Taveau," *William and Mary Quarterly,* 16 (April, 1936), 213.

20. Minor, *The Southern Literary Messenger,* p. 176.

21. Miller, p. 50.

22. *Ibid.*

23. Letter to John Esten Cooke, September 12, 1852, University of Virginia Library.

24. Minor, p. 172.

25. Jackson, p. 219.

26. *Ibid.,* p. 220.

27. James Grant Wilson, *Thackeray in the United States* (London, 1903), II, 128.

28. Mary N. Stanard, *Richmond: Its People and Its Story* (Philadelphia, 1923), pp. 137-38.

29. William Makepeace Thackeray, *The Letters and Papers of William Makepeace Thackeray* (London, 1946), III, 249.

30. Miller, pp. 53-54.

31. *Ibid.,* p. 54.

32. John R. Thompson, *Across the Atlantic* (New York, 1856), p. 17.

33. *Ibid.,* p. 33.

34. *Ibid.,* p. 36, and *SLM,* 22 (February, 1856).

35. *SLM,* 21 (June, 1855), 392. Editor's note to review.

36. Thompson, *Across the Atlantic,* pp. 120-21.

37. *Ibid.,* p. 364.

38. Phillips, II, 1541.

39. Thompson, *Across the Atlantic,* p. 390.

40. *SLM,* 25 (July, 1857), 71-73. Editor's Table.

41. Miller, p. 67. Also, in 1857 Thompson had applied for a professorship of Belles Lettres and Literature at South Carolina College.

42. John R. Thompson, *Virginia: A Poem* (Richmond, 1856).

43. Miller, pp. 69-71. Thomas Crawford, 1814-1857, born in New York but lived in Rome, where Thompson visited him in 1856, died before completing the statue of Washington. It is an equestrian statue and still stands

in front of the Capitol in Richmond. He is best known for his colossal figure of "Armed Liberty" for the Capitol at Washington.

44. William Gilmore Simms, *The Simms Letters* (Charleston, S. C., 1957), IV, 37.

45. *SLM,* 27 (September, 1858), 230.

46. Letter to George W. Bagby, June 9, 1860. University of Virginia Library.

47. Miller, p. 75. We do not know what Thompson was paid by MacFarlane and Fergusson. Bagby was paid three hundred dollars when he took over from Thompson, and White had paid Poe five hundred dollars a year. Thompson was probably somewhere between.

48. Letter to John R. Kennedy, March 22, 1860. Peabody Institute Collection.

49. Letter to John P. Kennedy, March 25, 1860. Peabody Institute Collection.

50. Miller, p. 76n.

51. Joseph Leonard King, Jr., *Dr. George W. Bagby: A Study of Virginian Literature* (New York, 1927), p. 78.

52. *SLM,* 30 (June, 1860), 466-67.

53. Letter to John P. Kennedy, May 26, 1860. Peabody Institute Collection.

54. *SLM,* 30 (June, 1860), 466.

Chapter Four

1. *SLM,* 30 (June, 1860), 466.

2. Letter to G. W. Bagby, 8 October 1858, University of Virginia Library.

3. Letter to G. W. Bagby, 11 October 1858, University of Virginia Library.

4. *SLM,* 14 (February, 1848), 123-28.

5. Jackson, p. 209.

6. *SLM,* 18 (December, 1853), 778.

7. Minor, p. 187.

8. *SLM,* 26 (May, 1848), 59-60.

9. *SLM,* 19 (April, 1851), 391.

10. Miller, p. 162.

11. *SLM,* 21 (October, 1855), 638.

12. *SLM,* 29 (August, 1859), 155.

13. *SLM,* 14 (August, 1848), 518.

14. *SLM,* 15 (February, 1849), 125.

15. *SLM,* 15 (September, 1849), 638. But cf. *SLM,* 14 (September, 1848), 575 and Miller, p. 169.

16. *SLM,* 15 (June, 1849), 373-74.

17. *SLM,* 16 (March, 1850), 239.

18. C. G. Eggleston, *Recollections of a Varied Life* (New York, 1910), p. 68.

19. The characteristics of the genteel tradition are derived from Richard Cary, *The Genteel Tradition in America, 1850-1875: with Selections from Unpublished Letters of Bayard Taylor, Richard Henry Stoddard, Edmund Clarence Stedman, and Thomas Bailey Aldrich,* Unpublished Doctoral Dissertation, Cornell University, 1952. Thompson was not always as neoClassical as he was while editor of the *Messenger.* Note, for example, his sentimental Romanticism in a college poem, "Despondency," [First stanza only is given, see Thompson, *Poems,* p. 229.]

> Oh! there are times when sorrows tinge the tablet of the soul,
> And o'er it naught but blasted hopes and gloomy visions roll,
> When all that passes 'round us and life's brightest prospects seem
> The relic of a thing that's gone! the shadow of a dream!

Indeed, he had several moments similar to this in later life and recorded them in verse, but they make up a small portion of his poetry.

20. *SLM,* 39 (August, 1859), 133-37.

21. Thompson, *Poems,* p. 79.

22. *SLM,* 14 (August, 1848), 555.

23. Thompson, *Poems,* p. 118.

24. *Ibid.,* p. 67.

25. *Ibid.,* p. 117.

26. *Ibid.,* p. 119.

27. *SLM,* 21 (March, 1855), 142.

28. Thompson was not alone in his opinion of Whitman's verse by any means. Paul H. Hayne, for example, wrote in a letter June 10, 1860, University of Virginia Library, "Your critique of *Mr. Walt Whitman* delighted me beyond measure. The *comparative* success of his work demonstrates the lowness both of *morals* and *taste* among even the better class of readers, & critics of the North. . . ." Where Thompson's review appeared I cannot discover.

29. Thompson, *Poems,* pp. 71, 240n. 17.

Chapter Five

1. Letter to J. P. Kennedy, May 26, 1860, Peabody Institute Collection. On the day before he wrote to Bagby, ". . . There is a good deal of drudgery to be done, but I think I should not mind this, if I thought I could stand Augusta. Don't, I beg you, mention it to a soul, for I should be laughed at, but this town is unbearable. Dull, provincial, hot, dusty, one-horse, fast asleep, out-of-the-world, everything that is fossilized [?] and stupid, why anybody lives here that can afford to live anywhere else puzzles me. But I shall grin and bear it, hoping for Baltimore against

hope....Letter to George W. Bagby, May 25, 1860, University of Virginia.

2. Letter to J. E. Cooke, May 24, 1860, University of Virginia.

3. Bagby, May 25, 1860, on back of letter cited in footnote 1 above.

4. *SLM,* 28 (April, 1859).

5. Letter to J. P. Kennedy, May 26, 1860, Peabody Institute Collection. But he also says in the same letter. "The duties of my office will involve some drudgery, but on the whole they will not amount to the work I have been compelled to do for several years past." His situation in Richmond is further described in a letter from his sister, "Then too, the thought that you are working more satisfactorially, in the pecuniary way, is a cheering one. Here you were constantly trammeled by debt, worried and harassed about money matters and almost always looking forward to the morrow with anxiety." Letter to J. R. Thompson from Mrs. Susan Quarles, June 26, 1860, University of Virginia.

6. *Southern Field and Fireside* (November 17, 1861), cited in Miller, p. 185.

7. Letter to J. R. Thompson from J. E. Cooke, July 26, 1861, University of Virginia.

8. In the July *Messenger* for 1860 there appeared this little puff:

The Poets and Poetry of the South, edited by Messrs John Esten Cooke and John R. Thompson, will be ready next fall, and will make the most attractive volume of the season. It will be published by Derby and Jackson. Some anxiety to know what Mr. Chas. A. Dana will think of the work is manifest. A great many are afraid he won't like it.

This note was almost certainly the work of Bagby, but he and Thompson felt in common a hostility toward Charles A. Dana as one whose snobbishness towards Southern writers was particularly offensive. In 1860 Dana was a critic for the New York *Tribune.* The identification of the publisher is something of a mystery, for Julia Moore Smith, writing in 1939, noted that her father, Van Moore, was working for Scribner's on a book titled *The Poets and Poetry of the South;* this may have been Thompson's book. A copy of Thompson's manuscript "Introduction" circulated about the offices of New York publishers for several years after this date.

9. Letter to J. P. Kennedy, February 9, 1861, Peabody Institute Collection. Henry W. Quarles had worked in the elder Thompson's store until he established his own store nearby at 21 Pearl Street. He also served on the Richmond city council in 1855-56. Also letter to J. P. Kennedy, January 4, 1861, Peabody Institute Collection. In May of the previous year, Thompson, who could not attend a meeting of the Old Dominion Society of New York, sent a poem which included this toast:

> Here North and South and East and West
> Are met in sweet communion —

Now drain the cup — this toast is best —
VIRGINIA AND THE UNION!

Thompson, *Poems,* p. 181.

10. Letter to J. P. Kennedy, February 26, 1861, Peabody Institute Collection.

11. Letter to J. P. Kennedy, May 16, 1861, Peabody Institute Collection.

12. *SLM,* 32 (April, 1861).

13. J. Cutler Andrews, *The South Reports the Civil War* (Princeton, N. J., 1970), p. 24 ff.

14. *Ibid.,* p. 26.

15. *Ibid.,* pp. 49-50.

16. Thompson, *Poems,* p. 36.

17. Andrews, p. 54.

18. *Ibid.,* p. 98.

19. *Ibid.,* p. 109.

20. *Ibid.,* p. 115.

21. *Memphis Daily Appeal,* August 6, 1861.

22. *Ibid.*

23. *Memphis Daily Appeal,* May 8, 1862.

24. Patton in Thompson, *Poems,* p. xxxiii.

25. Andrews, p. 163.

26. *Ibid.,* p. 171.

27. T. C. DeLeon, *Belles, Beaux and Brains in the Sixties* (New York, 1907), p. 203.

28. Andrews, p. 176.

29. *Ibid.,* p. 183.

30. *Ibid.,* pp. 184-85.

31. Stanard, p. 192. Also see Graves, p. 188. Also letter to J. R. Thompson from Lucy Ashton, August 3, 1862, University of Virginia. Lucy Ashton was probably Martha Davis of Essex County.

32. Letter to J. R. Thompson from Susan P. Quarles, September 25, 1865, University of Virginia. At this time Thompson lived at 802 Leigh Street; Washington, the painter, lived in the next block. He painted the picture three years after the poem, using local blacks and several Richmond society ladies. Mrs. Quarles names Lizzie Giles, Jennie Pegram, Mattie Paul, and Hetty Cary.

33. Thompson, *Poems,* pp. 4-5.

34. Andrews, p. 293. Francis Lawley was the fourth son of Lord Wenlock and at one time private secretary to Mr. Gladstone. He had a promising career in English politics until his gambling habits involved him in a scandal.

35. *Ibid.,* p. 187.

36. *Ibid.,* p. 188.

37. *Ibid.,* p. 220.

38. *Ibid.,* p. 386. In his own diary for January 28, 1864, Thompson wrote, "Some expenses for the past year, to show the cost of things: Paid for a breakfast for three people, $33, and one pound of butter $12, A shad $10. Gave my sister for wounded soldiers $50. Paragoric, $4. Bottle of brandy $50. Sent a note to Constance Cary, proceeds of a poem on the obsequies of Stuart, which note never received. Quart of milk, $4."

39. *Ibid.*

40. *Ibid.,* p. 391.

41. *Ibid.,* p. 392.

42. T. H. Baker, "Refugee Newspaper: *The Memphis Daily Appeal, 1862-1865," Journal of Southern History,* 29 (August, 1963), 339.

43. Letter to J. R. Thompson from William Gilmore Simms, January 10, 1863, University of Virginia.

44. Miller, p. 199. The early success of the *Southern Illustrated News* irritated Bagby who complained to his publishers that the *News* was taking subscribers away from the *Messenger.* In the *Messenger* he reported that "the paper...is said now to be making money at the rate of $50,000 per annum." *SLM,* 35 (November, 1862), 689. Bagby himself received $250 for his few contributions over a three-month period in 1863; see King, p. 102. In May, 1864, Paul H. Hayne was complaining that the *News* had not paid him "one red cent" for the poems published since January. Among the four or five poems Hayne sent during this period was a "Sonnet to J. R. T[hompson]." Letter to J. R. Thompson from Paul H. Hayne, May, 1864, University of Virginia. The financial troubles of the *News* may have been due largely to government restrictions on paper. In 1864 it often suspended publication because of government monopoly of paper and because of the conscription of printers.

45. Miller, p. 201.

46. *The Simms Letters,* IV, 392. Also *SLM,* 34 (January, 1862), 70.

47. Thompson, *Poems,* pp. 6-7.

48. Nevins, p. 408.

49. Thompson, *Poems,* pp. 11-12.

50. *Ibid.,* pp. 13-15.

51. *Ibid.,* p. 22.

52. Thompson, Diary, June 20, 1864.

53. *Ibid.*

Chapter Six

1. Miller, pp. 217-18, also see Patton in Thompson, *Poems,* p. xlii. Mason had been Special Commissioner of the Confederate States of America to Great Britain and Ireland until the Confederate Commission came to an end in 1863, after which he was designated "Commissioner to the Continent at Large." He frequently visited England and was on such a visit when Thompson arrived.

2. *Ibid.,* James Edward Macfarland of Petersburg, Va. had been secretary of the American legation at London before the war.

3.*The Unpublished London Diary of John R. Thompson,* University of Virginia Library. It has been published in part by Elizabeth C. Stoddard (Mrs. Richard H.): "Extracts from Diary of John R. Thompson," *Lippencott's Monthly Magazine,* 24 (November, 1888), 197-208; and by James Grant Wilson, "John R. Thompson and His London Diary, 1864-1865," *The Criterion* (November, 1901), pp. 8-13, 19-24, 23-25, 37-40.

4. Patton, p. xliii.

5. Thompson, *Diary.*

6. Letter to J. R. Thompson from Anne Thackeray, n.d. University of Virginia Library.

7. Thompson, *Diary.*

8. *Ibid.*

9. *Ibid.*

10. *Ibid.*

11. *Ibid.*

12. *Ibid.*

13. *Ibid.*

14. *Ibid.*

15. Miller, p. 250.

16. Thompson, *Diary.*

17. Thompson, *Diary.*

18. *Ibid.*

19. *Ibid.*

20. Letter to William Gordon McCabe from Anne Thackeray, February 15, 1874, University of South Carolina Library.

21. Graves, p. 189-90. Anne and Thompson kept up a correspondence for the rest of Thompson's life, but few of their letters seem to have survived — an unusual thing, since Thompson usually saved his letters. They may have been among the manuscript material given to Stoddard. Thompson sent her his poems and books he thought she would be interested in. She also invited him to a picnic in celebration of her twenty-ninth birthday — he was forty-three. In her letter to McCabe she wrote, "I have rarely in my life received a letter which touched me more. That my old friend should have thought of me went straight to my heart and filled my eyes. With gratitude and affection, his memory returns again and again, for I always felt that he was a true friend & one on whom I could rely."

22. Thompson, *Diary,* December 14, 1865.

23. Graves, p. 189.

24. Thompson, *Diary.* In her own diary Mrs. Emily Tennyson, Lady Tennyson, wrote, "June 29, 1866 — Next day Mr. Archibald Peel, Mr. Payne, Mr. Thompson, the Confederate. He, poor man, looks very sad and well he may, having lost his all in the war including the finest library in the South. One cannot but feel sorry for him." Unpub-

lished Journal, II, 64-65.

25. Thompson, *Diary.*

26. Miller, p. 260.

27. *Ibid.,* p. 261.

28. Letter to Barton Harrison, January 18, 1867, Harrison Collection, Library of Congress.

29. Letter to Barton Harrison, March 2, 1867, Library of Congress.

30. Miller, p. 263, letter dated April 8, 1867.

31. Letter to Hamilton Chamberlyne, n.d. University of Virginia Library.

32. Letter to George W. Bagby, February 25, 1868, University of Virginia Library.

33. Letter to J. R. Thompson from Paul Hamilton Hayne, 1869, University of Virginia Library.

34. Nevins, 408-09. DeLeon in *Belles, Beaux and Brains of the Sixties,* thinks little of Thompson's appointment on the *Post,* calling it "work that was rather made for him than useful to the paper." p. 203. But Eggleston, who was in a better position to judge wrote, "Bryant made him his intimate friend and appointed him to the office of literary editor of the *Evening Post,* which Mr. Bryant always held to be the supreme distinction possible to an American man of letters." p. 68. A little further on he noted, "J. R. Thompson was dead, and nobody had been found who could fill his place to Mr. Bryant's satisfaction....Mr. Bryant objected that they were all together men of the present, that they knew little or nothing of the older literature of our language, and hence, as he contended, had no adequate standards of comparisons in their minds." pp. 190-91. And Richard Cary observed of the *Post's* reputation at the time of Thompson's editorship, "It's literary taste was superior and more refined than that of its contemporaries." p. 288.

35. *Ibid.,* p. 408. Nevins gives this description of him as he appeared in New York, "a slight, gaunt man of forty-three [he was forty-six], the emaciation of whose face was partly concealed by his heavy beard, but who was clearly in bad health as in reduced circumstances....He was a kind of laureate of the Confederacy....His careful attention to dress, verging on foppishness, was less out of place in Bryant's office than it would have been in Greeley's or Dana's...."

36. *Evening Post,* January 26, 1869. William Cabell Rives was the father of Frank C. Rives, a classmate of Thompson at Virginia, and William C. Rives, Frank's younger brother; both were lifelong friends of Thompson.

37. Armistead C. Gordon, *Memories and Memorials of William Gordon McCabe* (Richmond, 1925), I, 318.

38. Nevins, pp. 409-10. Miller gives a list of the "insignificant" poets whose works Thompson published in the *Post,* but apologizes, saying he was not "given sufficient money....He did, however, secure brief poems

from some of the period's better poets, including Whittier, Bret Harte, Bayard Taylor, and Helen Hunt Jackson, and he used long selections of Bryant's translations. He also quoted from other journals: Longfellow, Whittier, Taylor, Mary E. Dodge, Margaret J. Preston," p. 277.

39. *Post,* December 23, 1868, and March 22, 1869.

40. *Ibid.,* August 16, 1869.

41. *Ibid.,* February 12, 1870.

42. *Ibid.*

43. *Ibid.,* February 17, 1870.

44. Nevins, p. 409.

45. Miller, p. 286.

46. *Ibid.,* p. 291. See *Appleton's,* July 2, 9, 23 and August 6, 1870.

47. *Post,* May 1, 1873. Bryant emphasized Thompson's ability as a conversationalist, saying, "His powers of conversation were of the very highest order, and in older societies than our own, where the charms of graceful and easy talk are cultivated and prized, he could have passed for one of the most agreeable 'society men'." Cooke in his tribute in the *Hearth and Home,* December 20, 1873, says much the same thing: "In Paris he would have taken his place, as of right, among the attractions of the literary *salons* and become famous among the wits of the wittiest city in Europe."

48. Letter from J. W. Davidson to Mrs. S. Quarles, May 10, 1873, University of Virginia Library.

49. Letter to Mrs. S. Quarles, February 5, 1871, University of Virginia Library.

50. Letter to William Gordon McCabe, May 7, 1871, Gordon, I, 313.

51. Gordon, I, 314.

52. Miller, p. 301.

53. Letter to J. R. Thompson from Mrs. S. Quarles, February 2, 1873, University of Virginia Library. Isaac Henderson wrote to McCabe, May 10, 1873, Gordon, I, 321, "It is now Saturday aft'n, 6 o'clock, and I embrace the very first moment I have had since the death of our dear friend, Thompson, to drop you a few lines in relation to his last hours....Mr. Thompson went to Colorado against my own judgment and the judgment of his friends, generally, but the Doctors ordered it and that was final...."

54. Gordon, I, 319.

55. Letter to Mrs. Isaac Henderson, April 17, 1873, University of Virginia Library.

56. Graves, p. 190.

57. *Post,* May 1, 1873. At the end of May, J. E. Cooke wrote to W. G. McCabe stresing Thompson's kindness, Gordon, I, 322-23,

Poor T. had his failings like all of us — the fact is, I don't think *any* of us will bear inspection with the microscope — but he had the great merit of being what everybody is not — *kind;* and my theory of life at forty-two is that there is nothing better in the world than kindness. Your critical estimate of Thompson is, I think, perfectly just, and very lucid, discriminative and yet cordial piece of writing....As a paragraphist and writer of sketches and articles Thompson was one of the best writers in America, and certainly among the very best literary editors, and most pointed, witty and finished poets of the lighter tone in *vers de societe*. He was, added to this, a very refined, delicate and honourable gentleman — very markedly so: and I mourn him along with his family.

58. Some hostility developed between Thompson's relatives and the Stoddards, and some rather harsh remarks were passed between them, particularly after Mrs. Stoddard published a part of Thompson's war diary. Of course, since Thompson had granted Stoddard the right to take, for his troubles, whatever from the collection he wished, the Quarleses could not fault him for keeping any or all of Thompson's books or manuscripts. Except as an ethical question, Stoddard was in the right, but his efforts were certainly not great. The most important loss was that of the handwritten fair copy of Thompson's poems. Patton collected all he could find, but we cannot be sure that all of Thompson's poems, even now, have been collected; certainly we cannot be sure that the poems Thompson wished to be remembered for are in the Patton collection.

Despite the fact that Thompson's library was burned, and some items were given away, when Stoddard sold what remained at auction, the sale included five hundred and forty-two books and one hundred and forty-two autographs.

Selected Bibliography

PRIMARY SOURCES

THOMPSON, JOHN R. *Across the Atlantic.* New York: Derby and Jackson, 1857. Based on Thompson's European journey in 1854, this book was burned before it could be issued. The only copy is in the University of Virginia Library.

————. *The Genius and Character of Edgar Allan Poe.* Richmond: Whitty and Rindfleish, 1929.

————. Letters and Papers in the Thompson Collection, University of Virginia Library.

————. *The Poems of John R. Thompson.* Ed. John S. Patton. New York: Scribner's. 1920. With the exception of one poem which is first published in the present volume, all of Thompson's known poetry is collected here.

SECONDARY SOURCES

ALLEN, HERVEY. *Israfel, the Life and Times of Edgar Allan Poe.* New York: Ferra & Rinehart, 1934. Allen's discussion of the Thompson-Poe friendship is the fairest to Thompson among the Poe biographies. Allen also establishes the fact that Poe was in Richmond for seven weeks in 1848.

ANDREWS, J. CUTLER. *The South Reports the Civil War.* Princeton, N.J.: Princeton University Press, 1970. Cutler Andrews draws a vivid picture of Civil War reporting, in which Thompson played a major part.

BAGBY, GEORGE W. *John Daniel's Latch Key: A Memoir of the Late Editor of the Richmond Examiner.* Lynchburg, Va.: J. P. Bell, 1868. Daniel was a friend of Thompson, who in 1848 offered to fight a duel with Poe.

BAKER, T. H. "Refugee Newspaper: *The Memphis Daily Appeal,* 1862–1865," *Journal of Southern History* 29 (August 1963), 327–39.

BEATY, JOHN O. *John Esten Cooke, Virginian.* New York: Columbia University Press, 1922. Some, but not much, of the friendship between Cooke and Thompson is discussed.

CAMPBELL, KILLIS. *The Mind of Poe and Other Studies.* Cambridge, Mass.: Harvard University Press, 1933. The "Poe-Griswold" essay in this book is the best treatment of the subject.

CARY, RICHARD. *The Genteel Tradition in America, 1850–1875: with Selections from Unpublished Letters of Bayard Taylor, Richard Henry Stoddard, Edmund Clarence Stedman, and Thomas Bailey Aldrich.* Unpublished Doctoral Dissertation, Department of English, Cornell University, 1952. Thompson knew and was influenced by these men and their critical theories.

COOKE, JOHN ESTEN. "John R. Thompson," *Hearth and Home,* December 20, 1873.

———. *Poe as Literary Critic.* Ed. N. B. Fagan. Baltimore, Md.: John Hopkins University Press, 1946.

DELEON, THOMAS COOPER. *Belles, Beaux and Brains of the Sixties.* New York: G. W. Dillingham, 1909. Thompson's social life is given some prominence in this book.

———. *Four Years in Rebel Capitals.* New York: Collier Books, 1962. Reissue.

EGGLESTON, G. C. *Recollections of a Varied Life.* New York: Henry Holt & Co., 1910. Eggleston was a writer and journalist who knew Thompson well and speaks of him in his autobiography.

GORDON, ARMISTEAD C. *Memories and Memorials of William Gordon McCabe.* Richmond: Old Dominion Press, 1925. Letters between McCabe and Thompson are quoted.

GRAVES, CHARLES MARSHALL. "Thompson, the Confederate," *Lamp* 30, No. 3 (October 1904), 181–90.

GRISWOLD, RUFUS W. *Passages from the Correspondence and Other Papers of Rufus W. Griswold.* Cambridge, Mass.: Harvard University Press, 1898. Includes most of the correspondence between Thompson and Griswold.

HOLLIDAY, CARL. *History of Southern Literature.* Port Washington, N.Y.: Kennikat Press, 1969. Gives a brief sketch of Thompson.

HUBBELL, JAY B. *The Last Years of Henry Timrod, 1864–1867.* Durham, N.C.: Duke University Press, 1941. Includes correspondence between Timrod and Thompson.

The Index, London, May 1, 1862–August 12, 1865. Thompson's letters appeared in *The Index* from the first; later he edited the periodical.

JACKSON, DAVID K. "Some Unpublished Letters of John R. Thompson and Augustin Louis Taveau," *William and Mary Quarterly* 16 (April, 1936), 206–21.

———. *The Contributors and Contributions to the Southern Literary Messenger.* Charlottesville, Va.: The Historical Publishing Co., 1936.

KING, JOSEPH L. *Dr. George W. Bagby: A Study of Virginia Literature, 1850–1880.* New York: Columbia University Press, 1927. As friend, correspondent, fellow editor, and journalist, Bagby was an important part of Thompson's life.

LINK, S. A. *Pioneers of Southern Literature.* Nashville, Tenn., and Dallas,

Texas: M. E. Church, South, Bingham & Smith, agents, 1903.

MALONE, HENRY T. "Atlanta Journalism during the Confederacy," *Georgia Historical Quarterly* 37 (September 1953), 210-19. Provides background information on the newspaper world. The *Memphis Appeal,* for which Thompson worked, is mentioned.

MANIERRE, WILLIAM R. "A Southern Response to Mrs. Stowe: Two Letters of John R. Thompson," *Virginia Magazine of History and Biography* 49 (January 1961), 83-92.

MCCABE, WILLIAM GORDON. "John R. Thompson," in *Library of Southern Literature.* Ed. E. A. Alderman, XII. Atlanta: Martin & Hoyt Co., 1907-1910. A long sketch of Thompson's career.

MILLER, JOHN C. *Building Poe Biography.* Baton Rouge: Louisiana State University Press, 1977. Miller doubts Thompson's reliability as a witness on Poe.

MILLER, JOSEPH RODDEY. *John Reuben Thompson: His Place in Southern Life and Literature.* Unpublished Doctoral Dissertation, Department of English, University of Virginia, 1930.

MINOR, B. B. *The Southern Literary Messenger, 1834-1864.* Washington: The Neale Publishing Co., 1905. The only complete history of the magazine, but often cryptic and never objective.

MOORE, RAYBURN S. *Paul Hamilton Hayne.* New York: Twayne Publishers, 1972.

MOTT, F. L. *American Journalism: A History of Newspapers in the U.S., 1690-1950.* New York: Macmillian, 1950. Contains a brief account of Thompson's connection with the *Evening Post.*

NEVINS, ALLAN. *The Evening Post: A Century of Journalism.* New York: Russell & Russell, 1968. Includes history of Thompson's work at the *Post.*

The New York Evening Post, 1868-1873.

OSTROM, JOHN WARD, *The Letters of Edgar Allan Poe.* New York: Gordian Press, 1966.

PAINTER, F. N. *Poets of the South: A Series of Biographical Critical Studies.* New York, Cincinnati, Chicago: American Book Co., 1903.

PARKS, EDD W. *Ante-Bellum Southern Critics.* Athens: University of Georgia Press, 1962. Good background and historical survey of the critical problems of the times.

PATTON, JOHN S., ed. *The Poems of John R. Thompson.* New York: Scribner's, 1920. Contains the nearest thing to a full-length biography — 50 pages — of Thompson in print.

PHILLIPS, MARY E. *Edgar Allan Poe: The Man.* Chicago, Philadelphia, Toronto: The John C. Winston Co., 1926. With this Poe biography the attack on Thompson begins in earnest. No author after Phillips accepted Thompson's statements on Poe as valid.

POE, EDGAR ALLAN. *The Complete Works of Edgar Allan Poe.* Ed. James A. Harrison. New York: AMA Press, 1965. Prints Thompson letters.

_____. *The Complete Poems of Edgar Allan Poe.* Ed. John H. Whitty. Boston and New York: Houghton Mifflin Co., 1911. Whitty's doubt of Thompson's reliability as a witness was hereafter used as an "authoritative source" to discredit Thompson.

_____. *The Works of the Late E. A. Poe.* Ed. Rufus W. Griswold. New York: J. S. Redfild, Clinton Hall, 1850.

PRICE, WARREN C. *The Literature of Journalism, An Annotated Bibliography.* Mineapolis: University of Minnesota Press, 1959.

QUINN, ARTHUR HOBSON. *Edgar Allan Poe: A Critical Biography.* New York: Appleton-Century Co., 1941. Prints the correspondence between Thompson and Griswold over Rosalie Poe's attempt to gain the copyright of Poe's *Tales and Poems.*

SIMMS, WILLIAM GILMORE. *The Simms Letters.* Charleston: University of South Carolina Press, 1957.

SMITH, JULIA MOORE. "A New Light on Poe?" *Southern Literary Messenger* 1, n.s. (September 1939) 575–91.

Southern Literary Messenger 13–30 (October 1847–June 1860).

STANARD, MARY NEWTON. *Richmond: Its People and Its Story.* Philadelphia: J. P. Lippincott, 1923. Provides interesting social background to Richmond in Thompson's time.

TERHUNE, MARY VIRGINIA. *Marion Harland's Autobiography: The Story of a Long Life.* London: Oxford University Press, 1946. Presents an early portrait of Thompson.

THACKERAY, WILLIAM M. *The Letters and Private Papers of William Makepeace Thackeray.* London: Oxford University Press, 1946. Gives brief account of Thompson-Thackeray friendship.

TRENT, WILLIAM P. *William Gilmore Simms.* New York: Haskell House, 1968.

WAGENKNECHT, EDWARD C. *Edgar Allan Poe: The Man behind the Mask.* New York: Oxford University Press, 1963.

WILSON, JAMES GRANT. *Thackeray in the United States.* London: Smith & Elder Co., 1903.

Index